COVENANTS *&* CARE

COVENANTS & CARE

Boundaries in
Life, Faith, and Ministry

GARY L. HARBAUGH

REBECCA LEE BRENNEIS

RODNEY R. HUTTON

FORTRESS PRESS

MINNEAPOLIS

COVENANTS AND CARE
Boundaries in Life, Faith, and Ministry

Book design by Joseph Bonyata.

Cover design by Mike Mihelich.

Library of Congress Cataloging-in-Publication Data
Harbaugh, Gary L., 1936– .
    Covenants and care : boundaries in life, faith, and ministry /
Gary L. Harbaugh, Rebecca Lee Brenneis, Rodney R. Hutton.
      p.   cm.
    Includes bibliographical references.
    ISBN 0-8006-2988-4 (alk. paper)
    1. Clergy. 2. Pastoral theology. 3. Covenants—Religious
aspects—Christianity. I. Brenneis, Rebecca Lee, 1961– .
II. Hutton, Rodney R., 1948– . III. Title.
BV4011.H334 1998
253'.2—dc21
                                 98-9525
                                    CIP

Manufactured in the U.S.A.   AF1-2988

02   01   00   99   98   1   2   3   4   5   6   7   8   9   10

CONTENTS

ACKNOWLEDGMENTS

Many have contributed to our understanding of covenants and care. We have grown as persons and pastors through the faithful, covenantal care of others. In particular, we remember the love and cherish what we have learned about family covenants through Joanne Ullrich Brenneis, Ethel Zwanziger, and Margaret Carns Harbaugh.

In ministry, the support of colleagues is a true blessing. We thank our colleagues at Trinity Lutheran Seminary, especially Dennis A. Anderson and James M. Childs Jr. We are grateful for the support of our Bishop, William B. Trexler, and for supportive colleagues on the staff of the Office of the Bishop, Florida-Bahamas Synod, and of the Division for Ministry, ELCA. We also found helpful the suggestions of our colleagues at the Florida-Bahamas synodical Conference on Ministry, where we first shared our understanding of how the biblical concept of covenant relates to pastoral ministry.

At Fortress Press, we acknowledge the helpful support and assistance of Marshall D. Johnson, J. Michael West, Henry F. French, Sandra M. Burrowes, and Joseph Bonyata.

PREFACE

This book is about covenants and care. It is about and for ministers who pastorally care for God's covenant people.

Christians live in a covenant relationship with God. As leaders of the Christian community, ministers proclaim the gospel that, through Christ, we are all part of the new covenant community.

What does it mean to be in covenant? How does being in covenant help us identify what is truly pastoral care? What are the implications of being in covenant for care of a congregation, of family and friends, and of ourselves? How does not attending to a covenant relationship, or breaking covenant, affect ministry? What are appropriate and helpful steps ministers can take to live the covenant they proclaim and nurture the covenants they make? What are some of the early signs of difficulty that can signal the need for a minister to take preventive steps to avoid a breach of covenant and care?

This book is written with the conviction that ministers want to be faithful in covenant and caring, and with the confidence that sometimes it only takes an encouraging word or two to assist a colleague along the way.

Pastor Leon* is one such pastor who could use a helpful and supportive word as he struggles with issues of covenant and care. Although every situation is unique, there are some things about Pastor Leon's experiences that could apply to all ministers. As we consider various aspects of covenants and care, we shall refer back to Pastor Leon, so perhaps it will help to introduce him at this time.

*Pastor Leon, Pastor María, Florence, and others mentioned in the following case study are not actual persons; the case study is intended to be true to life, but the case material is not true life and no reference to any actual individual or situation is intended or to be inferred.

PART ONE

COVENANT & MINISTERS

1

COVENANT & GRACE

PASTOR LEON AND COVENANTS

Portrait of a Pastor

Pastor Leon is forty-two years old. Leon and his spouse, Leah, have a fourteen-year-old daughter and a nine-year-old son. Leon graduated from seminary when he was twenty-eight. Prior to seminary, he followed in his father's footsteps and earned a bachelor's degree in business administration. For the first two years after college, Leon was a manager trainee in a financial institution. While he enjoyed his working relationships with the rest of the staff, Leon was not certain he wanted to live with the competitiveness he saw in the corporate world. One day a pastor he met at a community meeting observed that business and administrative skills are useful for pastors. When the pastor asked Leon if he had ever considered the ministry, Leon began to think of a vocational change. Leon's parents were concerned that he was giving up a promising economic future, but they were supportive because the church had always been an important part of Pastor Leon's family life, and Leon felt God's call.

At the seminary, Leon especially liked biblical studies. He found Hebrew easier than Greek, so he gravitated toward the Old Testament. Seminary did not prove too much of a financial hardship because he was offered a work-study position in the seminary's business office. During his senior year he began to talk about marriage with Leah, a young woman he met when he went back home to visit his parents on his first Spring break from seminary. Leon and Leah married just before he took his first call to a congregation.

Leon is now in his third congregation. He served as an assistant minister for three years and then served in a small, rural congregation for five years prior to accepting the call to Leesville Community Church. Leesville Community Church is the only interdenominational church in the area, although there are a number of other Protestant churches, a synagogue, and a Roman Catholic parish.

One by one, Leon has seen turnover in the Ministers Association. Leon has not attended the ministers' meetings as regularly as he had since his closest colleague was transferred and Leon's congregation began experiencing conflict. There is now only one other minister in the community, Pastor María, with whom Leon feels any rapport. María is also a second-career person in ministry. She is older than Leon and has three grown children and two young grandchildren. Leon was pleased when he learned that María shared his interest in biblical theology, especially the Old Testament.

Except for one seminar, Pastor Leon has had little time in the past year for continuing education. His congregation's membership has declined since the announcement that Leesville's major industry was being dramatically downsized and the word leaked out that the corporation was considering relocating to another state. For two years members of the congregation have had to live with that threat, and things in the congregation have been going downhill. Because so many of Pastor Leon's 150 remaining members are dependent on that one industry, there has been increased financial pressure placed on many members. Offerings have been decreasing, and a year ago the part-time church secretary had to be let go. Threats of industrial relocation continue and were mentioned when Pastor Leon's salary was capped at the last annual meeting. The life situation for Leon's family was further complicated two months ago when Leah's job was cut to half salary and her working hours switched to evenings.

As a possible way to deal with their financial pressure, Leon mentioned to Leah that one of the members of the congregation expressed an interest in starting a business to locate employment options for community members who have lost their jobs. With the pastor's business administration background and community connections, the member proposed a joint venture with the pastor that could include Leah as office manager. Leon is seriously considering this possibility especially because, if the membership gets much smaller, he doubts that the congregation will be able to continue his full salary.

Leah is not so sure she wants to continue to work if her present job is phased out. She is concerned about the needs of their daughter, Lisa, who is turning more and more to her mother as she becomes a young woman. Lisa used to be closer to her father. In the rural parish, when Lisa was seven, she remembers her father being home a lot more, and she misses the playful times they used to have. Now it seems that all her father does is work. Even when he is at home, their communication has become much less frequent and more awkward during the past year or two. Leah is also concerned about their son, Leon Jr. (who likes to be called Leo to keep from being confused with his dad). Leo complains that every time his father says he will come to his ball games, some emergency seems to come up that keeps Dad away. Leo wishes his father could be like other fathers, who seem to care more about the interests of their sons. Leah tries to reassure her children that their father really does care but inwardly she also feels neglected. Communication with Leon has been reduced to talking about those practical necessities that can no longer be let go, such as when Leo's teacher last week requested a parent's conference to discuss Leo's declining grades. Leah feels torn between her husband's insistence that she help out with finances and her growing concern that she will have no help from Leon in picking up the slack at home.

A Pastor under Stress

Leon is trying not to let it show, but he is experiencing a lot of stress trying to keep on top of things in the congregation. He does not know how to deal with community forces over which he has no control. He knows that family life is not as good as it used to be, but he is so tired at the end of the day that he has no more energy to take care of problems at home. He welcomes those evenings when Lisa and Leo are already in their rooms when he comes home, although he regrets that he feels that way. He is even glad when Leah has already gone to bed. It's just that he is so worn out that he is afraid he will appear indifferent. A drink or two and the late night movie give him a little relief, but sometimes he is too tired to last through the movie. He believes that drinking helps relax the muscles in his chest. For a while he thought he might be having heart trouble, but the pain seems to go away after his second drink.

This afternoon, Leon is thinking about a female parishioner who left a message on the church answering machine. Florence (Flo) was new to the faith when she joined the church last year. She was dynamic, cheerful, and very positive in her outlook—overall an uplifting person to be around. Flo is career oriented and never married. Her apartment is comfortably homey and she has a great love for children. Shortly after she became a member, Flo volunteered to organize a latchkey program for children in the congregation and the surrounding neighborhood. She thought it would help parents who had to work Saturdays due to shifting economic conditions. Flo worked closely with Pastor Leon on that project.

Two months ago, Flo's father died. She had been very close to her father and she asked Pastor Leon to help her with her grief following his death. As Leon listened to her feelings, he became more in touch with his own feelings of loss. He began to realize how different his life has become. When he first became a pastor, he had time for personal Bible study and prayer. Now he has time to read Scripture only when preparing for preaching or teaching. He hopes God understands that when you work fourteen-hour days your *life* has to be your prayer. He has even recently begun to wonder whether or not he should continue in ministry at Leesville—or anywhere else. Maybe that business venture would be the answer.

Leon hesitates raising any of his inner questions to Leah because almost every discussion results in her bringing up the issue of his not ever being at home. Their intimate life has eroded over the past six months due to his fatigue and Leah's dissatisfaction with him. Leon also feels disconnected from his children. He misses the earlier playful years with his daughter and feels guilty when he senses his son's disappointment with him. While it made him aware of his own losses, Leon felt useful and needed by Flo in her time of loss, and she has let him know repeatedly how very much she appreciated his availability and comforting words.

Today has been particularly stressful. The receipts for this month are the lowest so far, and the treasurer told Leon that he will have to make a very pessimistic report at the council meeting tomorrow. Leah has to work tonight, so at least he won't have to tell her that the church finances are looking their worst yet.

As Leon is sitting in his office wondering what to do, the telephone rings. "Leesville Community Church," he says. "Oh, Pastor Leon, this is Flo. I'm so glad you're there. I'm feeling a little down. Maybe you remember, tomorrow would have been my father's birthday and I'm going to drive over to see Mom. I was wondering if you could come by tonight to give me some ideas about how to support Mom tomorrow—that is, if you don't have to work. To thank you, I made something special for dessert and I just discovered a great liqueur that goes with it." Leon doesn't have a meeting. He takes a deep breath. . . .

A Return to Covenant

Before we return to Pastor Leon's office to see how he responds to Flo's telephone call, let's turn back the clock about six months for some additional personal history. At that time, Leon's pastoral colleague, Pastor María, was telling him that her presbytery was sponsoring an Old Testament seminar on covenant theology. Until then Leon was unaware that he and María shared a common interest in the Old Testament. They decided to attend the seminar together, and on the two-hour drive to the seminar site they became better acquainted.

The church in Leesville was María's first parish. She was struggling to establish her identity in a congregation that had never before had a female pastor nor a pastor with Anglo-Hispanic heritage. She was also divorced, which was uncomfortable for some members of her congregation. María told Leon that, with the help of a professional therapist, she had worked through her personal issues about being divorced, which had occurred after her children were in college and about three years before she went to seminary. On the other hand, being a single female in her first pastoral role presented many challenges and, being single, there was no one at home to provide understanding and support.

By the time they arrived at the seminar, Leon and María realized that it might be helpful for them to get together as colleagues from time to time—if only they could find the time in their demanding schedules! The seminar was María's first since becoming a pastor nearly two years ago. It had been even longer for Leon since he had attended a biblical seminar. He sighed wearily as he told María how regular Bible study and prayer had once been an everyday discipline for him—but seldom was there time any more! María could easily identify with not having enough time.

The seminar's focus on covenant at first represented to Leon and María a welcome retreat from what was going on in their lives back in Leesville. While at first the seminar seemed like only a review of what had been taught at seminary, it also became an opportunity to explore a number of stimulating new thoughts. Leon gave the seminar leader his full attention as the question was posed, "Is the idea of covenant useful for us today and, if so, what does it mean for us to be in covenant?"

COVENANT IN BIBLICAL THEOLOGY

In the 1940s and 1950s the word "covenant" came to be considered the principal word to describe the dynamic relationship between God and God's people.[1] It is at least clear that Abraham and Sarah were from very early times regarded as recipients of God's covenantal promise.[2] Early prophetic writings also recalled that Israel was known by Yahweh in a special way that set Israel apart from all other nations. "You only have I known of all the families of the earth" (Amos 3:3). Hosea speaks of Israel's relationship with Yahweh as one that can be characterized by the name of one of his children, 'ammi, "my people." Hosea could speak of Yahweh as Israel's maker (8:14), the one who knew Israel intimately (13:5).

While the earliest prophetic traditions did not think of Israel's relationship with God only in terms of a covenant, they clearly believed that there existed a special bond between the people of God and their God whom they knew personally as Yahweh. The prophet Jeremiah spoke of this relationship both in terms of the old covenant and the new covenant into which God's people were being called (Jer. 31:31-34).[3]

When Leon heard the seminar leader ask, "Is the idea of covenant useful for us today and, if so, what does it mean for us to be in covenant?" he thought about what was going on in his congregation. He realized that in recent years neither he nor his congregational layleaders seemed to have the kind of confidence that the prophet Jeremiah did. In the middle of financial pressures and stress, it was hard to feel a special bond with God. More often than not, Leon and most of the congregation identified not with Jeremiah's covenant thinking, but with his Lamentations!

Now, six months after attending the seminar, Leon is feeling even more frustrated and helpless. Each Sunday at the end of worship he pronounces the benediction, but he is not experiencing the peace (shalom) of the Lord and he doubts that many congregational members are.

How might Leon apply understandings about covenant to his life situation and ministry? He is at a point in his life and ministry where not only his congregants but he is also very much in need of care. What does covenant have to do with care?

A primary characteristic of a covenant is that it has to do with relationship. To think covenantally about Christian caring is to think about care as it relates to the three relationships at the heart of Shalom: self, others, and God.

For Christians who believe that life itself is a gift from God, entering into a covenant of care for self, for others, and for God is one way to thank God for what we have received. While we cannot keep a covenant by our own reason or strength, we trust that God will provide the means whereby we can at least take some steps in the direction of living within a covenant of care.

Covenant and Care of Self

Leon is in a very difficult spot. His personal and family life is disintegrating at the same time that he has major vocational questions about continuing at Leesville. He even wonders if he should continue being a pastor. He is needed everywhere and he comes home so exhausted that he is glad when others are already in bed so he doesn't have to give anything more of himself. His body is showing signs of buckling under the pressure. He is assuming that his chest pains are stress-related because they are not so severe when he drinks alcohol. Leon is using alcohol to reduce his stress and needs more than one drink to feel relaxed. His desire to avoid additional family demands if at all possible and his escape into alcohol are coping mechanisms that frequently result in a negative outcome.

A covenant of care with oneself is a faithful response to the gift of our personhood. Some ministers are uncomfortable with the idea of self-care, thinking that self-care is self-centered or selfish, unfaithful, and self-absorbed. For those unable to think comfortably of caring for oneself, another covenantal way to understand self-care is to think of self-care as being *for the sake of ministry*. The Bible records how even Jesus would get away from the crowds for a while, perhaps to a mountaintop, prior to returning to the valley to press on with his ministry. The getting *away* seemed to be for the sake of getting *on*.

Self-care for the sake of ministry requires that we learn to meet more effectively the unmet needs that affect ministerial health and wellness. Some of those needs were identified in 1990 when Mark Galli reported the results of a survey in *Leadership* magazine. The survey had invited readers of *Leadership* to name the most helpful articles the magazine had published in the previous decade (the first ten years of the magazine's life). Galli reports, "Twenty of the top thirty articles from our first ten years dealt with the demands ministry places on a pastor's personal life."[4]

What are some of the most significant problems ministers face?[5] Time pressures, over-extension, and the lack of a sense of accomplishment are among the problems ministers commonly identify. In addition, some who work closely with ministers also observe loneliness, feelings of inadequacy, and a lost sense of meaning.[6] Still others point out problems associated with stress from constant interpersonal contact and continually increasing effort to meet the rigorous demands and expectations of ministry.[7]

Craig W. Ellison and William S. Mattila in 1983 reported the results of a *Leadership* survey of 1,000 readers in which respondents as a whole identified stress, frustration, and feelings of inadequacy as major problems. These major problems were intercorrelated in statistically significant ways. For example, *stress* was correlated with *time demands*. Lack of time correlated with ministers having no time to be alone and to unrealistic expectations of their own. *Frustration* was fueled by difficulties in motivating people, unfulfilled dreams, unmet ministry goals, and unrealistic expectations of their own. *Feelings of inadequacy* were related to defensiveness when personal views are questioned, time demands, and difficulty in motivating people. *Spiritual dryness* related to constant time demands and unrealistic expectations of their own. *Fear of failure* was associated with unrealistic expectations of their own and key people not sharing their vision. *Loneliness and isolation* were related to the lack of an intimate confidant with whom they could share their needs, little understanding from denominational leaders, and unrealistic expectations of their own.

The common thread Ellison and Mattila saw running through each of the most pressing problems had to do with expectations:

> Unrealistic expectations promote constant time demands. . . . It appears that frustration, depression, and feelings of inadequacy . . . are also produced in part by the failure to meet expectations. . . . Therefore, it seems to us that idealism and high expectations are a common base for the most frequently indicated problems, often due to a perceived gap between what is desired and what is achieved in the specific context of ministry.[8]

If you are personally experiencing any of the thoughts and feelings of those who responded to these surveys and studies of ministers, then it would be appropriate to consider entering into a covenant of care for yourself—for the sake of your ministry. There is a rhythm that God set in motion in our lives by breathing into us the breath of life. We need to breathe in and out, out and in. Often the expectations of ministry are so great that we breathe out and out and out and out. It is important that we also remember to breathe in, to take a refreshing deep breath, to catch our breath, to reflect on the fact that we are only human. Remembering that we need to breathe in as well as out is also a reminder that we are mortal and finite and therefore limited. We are not God. It is faithful for us, when it seems like the world depends only on us, to let go and let God.[9]

Covenant and Care of Others

The concerns *Leadership* identified with ministerial health and wellness also extend to a minister's marriage and family life in those denominations with married clergy. In 1992 David Goetz reported the results of a survey of 748 pastors on family matters.[10] To the question "On the whole, do you think being a pastor is a benefit or hazard to your family life?" 57 percent said being a pastor benefited family life, which left 43 percent thinking that being a pastor was hazardous to home life! On their marriages, only 55 percent said they were "very satisfied" with their marriages. Even fewer ministers (31 percent) were "very satisfied" with their family life and only 25 percent thought ministers' spouses were "very satisfied" with family life. More than half the respondents identified with the following problems: 81 percent insufficient time together, 71 percent use of money, 70 percent income level, 64 percent communication difficulties, 63 percent congregational expectations, 57 percent differences over use of leisure, and 53 percent difficulty in raising children. That time pressure was the number one problem, says Goetz, is "virtually unchanged from a *Leadership* survey in 1988, in which 83 percent of pastors surveyed listed it as the number one problem."

The kinds of problems listed above are interrelated. Time pressure usually results in families having less time to spend together as a family, and less time together can lead to misunderstandings and miscommunications, which can emerge symptomatically as disagreements over how to use money and what little leisure time exists, and so on. In other words, interpersonally unsatisfying cycles can be precipitated when there just isn't time to take care of our primary relationships.

The Hebrew understanding of Shalom, however, gives us reason to take the time. Shalom, biblically, means having a right relationship in a trinity of life's dimensions, leading to a peace which only God can give. One of those dimensions is self. Shalom means having a right relationship with oneself, and so self-care is not only appropriate for ministerial health and wellness, it is essential for shalom.

Shalom cannot be experienced, however, only by having a right relationship with oneself. No one could be a solitary Israelite, no matter how well that individual took care of himself or herself. An Israelite was only an Israelite in relationship to the rest of the people of Israel. Relationship with others—a right relationship—was and is essential for the shalom of God's people. That shalom relationship with others extends beyond our immediate family to the congregational family and the community around us, but it cannot exist in the way God intended it if it does not include our primary relationships.

It is sad when we hear that a child of a minister has become alienated from the church. For some of those daughters and sons, it is because they believe that, through the church's incessant demands on the minister's time, the church took away their parent. The increasing number of ministers' marriages that end in divorce reflects society's standards not only in the ease and acceptability of divorce, but also the greater social support for persons who are not happy living with what is left over when their spouse comes home from work. Some minister's spouses accept that they will have little couple time and try to make that time high quality to compensate for less quantity. Even those spouses who agree to less at the beginning can, over time, weary of giving up so much couple and family time, and are more likely to become frustrated and dissatisfied when the promised high-quality time begins to deteriorate into simply time that is left over.

All of us need to take responsibility for our use of time in relation to the church, because the church cannot in fact take time away unless we choose to give it. Often the element of choice seems to be missing, leaving a minister with a desperate sense of never having enough time and everyone wanting more and no one really satisfied. It is so easy, when a minister is feeling caught in the time bind, to assume that those at home, those who love the minister the most, will understand the most if the minister is not available for them.

A covenant of care, not only with oneself but also with others, cannot faithfully be made at the expense of a minister's primary relationships. Because family and friends are the most likely to understand if we neglect them, for that reason these are the relationships that most need our intentional nurture and care. If as ministers we are tempted to break Shalom with others by neglecting the relational dimension of life, that temptation will be the greatest where our neglect will be tolerated the longest. In family life these weeds show up as symptoms. A spouse may become anxious or depressed or ill, children may act out at school or with peers. Married or unmarried, ministers may also strain their valued friendships if they do not nurture those friendships. Not all symptoms are signs of neglect, of course, as there are other reasons a spouse or a child or a friend may be unhappy. It is wise, however, to remember that our covenant with ourselves is incomplete without a corresponding covenant with others, beginning with those with whom we are closest. To enter into a covenant with others, as with oneself, is to be faithful in our covenant with God.

Covenant and Care with God

A Shalom right relationship with oneself and with others is only fully completed within the context of a right relationship with God. The Israelite is an Israelite only in relation to the rest of Israel, but Israel is a people only in relationship with God (Hos. 1:9, 2:23).

Studies of ministerial health and wellness suggest that time pressure is a pervasive factor in a minister's life and home and that expectations underlie much of that time pressure. It would be interesting to know whether the spiritual dryness and lost sense of meaning that also appear in those studies is the *result* of trying to meet time pressures and incessant demands or whether spiritual dryness and a lost sense of meaning *cause* a minister to be vulnerable to those time pressures and especially the inappropriate expectations.

From a Shalom perspective, we may consider that the most important relationship to have right is our relationship with God. Out of that vertical relationship, which is the source of life and health, will flow life and health in our relational and personal life.

The key, of course, is knowing what makes our relationship with God right. The answer to such a question depends on how we ask the question. To say what makes our relationship with God right is likely to lead to an increased sense of responsibility to be faithful in doing everything that there is to be done, everything that God calls us to do. If we are good and faithful servants, then we may think our relationship with God will be right.

However, to have a right relationship with God that depends on what *we* do is not the gospel. The Law demands that we live up to our obligations. The gospel proclaims a different word. The correct way to ask the question is not what makes our relationship with God right, but *who* makes it right. The gospel is good news because it proclaims that God has made our relationship right through the giving of God's Son to us (John 3:16).

To have a right relationship with God, to experience God's Shalom, we have only to receive God's gift of Shalom through Christ Jesus. Even the ability to receive such a gift is itself a gift of the Holy Spirit. Nothing, ultimately, depends on what we do, but on what God has done and does for us. God loves us just the way we are. We are free to be who we are in Christ instead of having to do anything to earn God's love. What good news! To not *have* to do anything! To not *have* to meet any expectations!

To not *have* to do anything leaves us free to choose to do the best we can, not as if our life depends on it (Christ has taken care of that!), but because we want to say "thank you" to God with our lives and through what we do. Not out of obligation but out of gratitude, we thank God for our personal life by taking care of ourselves. We thank God for our relationships, especially those nearest and dearest, by taking care of those whom we love. We thank God for God through worship and praise and prayer, through witnessing to others who do not know the freedom that only God can give, through caring for God's people in the church and in the community, through mission and ministry.

This trinity of relationships—with self, with others, and with God—is at the heart of Shalom. A covenant of care with each is not something we *have* to make, it is something we want to live as a way of saying "thanks be to God."

FORMING A COVENANT GROUP

As one way to express thankfulness to God, we invite you to consider finding a few other ministers with whom you can form a covenant group. A covenant group is a group of colleagues. The leadership may naturally fall to one of the group members or rotate among the members of the group. Another option that some denominations have found helpful in peer support is to have a group facilitator, someone who is familiar with group dynamics and group processing, such as a hospital chaplain or Christian counselor.[11]

The purpose of the covenant group is to provide mutual support and accountability. We might think of that support and accountability in terms of living Shalom and of promise keeping.

Living Shalom

It is not easy for us in the midst of ministerial pressures and demands to live Shalom. No one understands the expectations on ministers as well as ministers themselves. That makes it possible for a peer group to be of mutual support and consolation, each member of the group knowing what it is like and each committed to being there for the others.

Those groups that are the most helpful to ministers, however, are not groups where the ministers spend all their time lamenting their lot in life. Lamentation can be a healthy expression, as the Psalmist has taught us. But lament is not an end in itself. It is a cry that others hear and perhaps can identify with, but fundamentally it is a cry to God. God's response to us, through the other members of the covenant group, is not the response of Job's comforters, those who wondered aloud what Job had done to deserve what he got (Job 11). God's response, through the group, is true comfort and consolation, expressed by helping the lamenter tell the story, think the thoughts, feel the feelings, and say what needs to be said.

For lament not to be an end in itself, the covenant group does more than provide a place for safe ventilation. Besides the psalms of lament, many other psalms express praise or thanksgiving, proclaiming what God has done, is doing, and will do. In fact, it is quite characteristic of the psalms that such joyful outbursts of celebration already intrude into the lament psalms themselves, as the psalmist in distress already has an astounding confidence and trust in God's ability and willingness to deliver (for example, Ps. 22).

Translated into covenant group action, the way to keep lament from being its own end is to help the lamenting one to begin to see the situation from the perspective of how God might be able to transform what looks like a dead end into a new lease on life. The resurrection power of God continues to bring new life out of the old when each day both curse and blessing, death and life are set before us and, by the grace of God, we choose life!

Covenant Keeping

Choosing life is empowered by God's choosing life for us and is expressed in our *living* our thanks to God by nurturing right relationships with others as well as with ourselves. The second way in which a covenant group can be helpful is by holding each other mutually accountable for balancing lament with praise, honest expressions of thought and feeling with prayerful confidence in God's continuing care and ability to bring light from darkness, life from death.

In recent years, there has been renewed appreciation for the importance of promise keeping. Promise Keepers is indeed the name of one group that is committed to faithfulness in life and living. More important even than our promise keeping, however, is our realization that the primary promise keeper is God. It is because of God's faithfulness in keeping promises that we are free to keep our promises out of love rather than out of fear of the consequences of our not keeping them.

A covenant group can be helpful when members slip into thinking about *what* makes a right relationship possible, rather than *who* makes Shalom possible. A covenant group can be helpful when it looks like everything seems to be dependent on us and what we do, rather than on God and the power of the Resurrection. The covenant group can be helpful in bringing the group to a remembrance of our Baptism, itself a gift that involves a dying and rising again (Rom. 6), a dynamic rhythm that ever brings forth the new through God's transforming grace.

Grace-full Group Guidelines

For those seeking to establish a covenant group, the guidelines used to develop collegiality and mutual growth in one of the denominations are worthy of note.[12] Some of the objectives of a collegial group are:

To help clergy understand and accept their need for peer affirmation and for mutual accountability in personal life and in conducting public ministry, to offer clergy a place where they may temporarily set aside the role of "pastoral caregiver" and focus on their own care, health, and wholeness, to provide a safe place where clergy (or other leaders) can speak honestly about their personal or pastoral concerns and receive feedback in an informed and non-judgmental atmosphere, to reduce some of the intellectual, spiritual, and role-connected isolation experienced by many leaders.

To develop covenant groups that provide mutual support and accountability, some suggest monthly meetings—but preferably not in the evening when the work of the day has sapped most of the energy of group members. At the least, there should be twenty-four hours of meetings annually—for example, eight three-hour meetings or six four-hour meetings, but meeting for a long enough period of time for all participants to be heard and transforming support to be given. Ideally, the group is no smaller than five persons nor more than eight, which allows enough interaction, yet is not too many participants for individual attention. The place of covenant group meeting should be comfortable and private, away from the intrusion of telephones and beeping pagers.

A group covenant, a written covenant that each member signs, is desirable. A sample covenant follows:

Covenant

I declare my intention to be a faithful participant in my covenant group.

As a faithful participant, I will attend every group meeting. If an emergency should prevent my attending, I will notify another group member or the facilitator.

I will recognize that the central purpose of our meeting is to develop a spirit of collegiality and mutual growth that will undergird and enhance our ministries.

I will hold confidential all that occurs in our group meetings, even from those outside the group whom I feel I can trust.

I will communicate honestly about my experiences in ministry, even those that seem like failures, recognizing that these are the experiences from which I can most readily enlarge my understanding of my role in ministry.

I will demonstrate respect for my colleagues by letting them see me as I am, not solely as I would like to be. I will demonstrate trust by allowing my colleagues their right to their privacy, when they so choose.

I will seek opportunities to affirm and support my colleagues.

I will recognize the presence of God with us in all of our doings—in our struggles and our perplexities, in our joy and in our laughter—not confining my sense of God's presence to our times of worship, but recognizing that the spirit of God is continually among us two or three who meet to search for ways to enhance ministry in our part of God's world.

_____

Covenant Group Member

_____

Date

The value of a written covenant is that it represents a commitment to mutual support and a recognition of the kind of accountability that is essential to the development of trust within a group. If the group is to be faithful as a covenant group, then the characteristics of God's covenant with us are ones that need to be manifest in the group, particularly the characteristics of promises made and promises kept. With God seen as the primary promise maker (and promise keeper), the members of the covenant group are free to show their thankfulness through the development of graceful group guidelines that are followed not by obligation, but by desire to be there for each other as God is always there for us. Through our mutual commitment and faithfulness, God's care and faithfulness is all the more clearly revealed, and even the darkest valley through which one of the group members is walking is walked with the confidence that we do not walk alone.

2

COVENANT & TRANSITIONS

TRANSITIONS IN MINISTRY

Who Am I Now?

Pastor Leon finds himself at a transition point in ministry. Transitional times are opportunities for growth. In order to manage this transition with integrity and wisdom it is prudent for Pastor Leon to take a look at who he is at this time in his life. What does he bring to his situations that enhances or interferes with healthy relationships at home and in the parish?

Self-esteem is a key issue in the health of an individual. What do we think about ourselves? Do we define ourselves in terms of what we learned about ourselves through family members? In terms of how God sees us?

In the best of worlds we learn that we are lovable in our biological families, that we are worthy just because. Unfortunately, if our family of origin does not provide this kind of acceptance and unconditional love, we may go to great lengths to prove our value through what we accomplish. The conditional reward for such work is temporary, so we need more and more tasks to keep a sense of self-worth. This can result in overachievement, perfectionism, compulsivity, codependence, sheer exhaustion, and burnout.

Rather than counting on our achievements to give us worth, Christians look to God as the source of our self-worth. We are worthy because of God's covenant with us to love and sustain us. Jesus is asked, "Teacher, which is the great commandment in the law?" Jesus responds, citing the words of the covenant relationship summarized in the *shema*: "You shall love the Lord your God with all your heart, with all your soul, and all your mind. This is the great and first commandment." Then, citing the command of Leviticus 19:18, Jesus adds, "And the second is like it, you shall love your neighbor as yourself" (Deut. 6:5 and Matt. 22:34 ff.). This passage affirms love of self, which is also a faithful response to the love of God.

We learn how to love others by accepting God's unconditional love for us. In this way our identity with God defines our worth because our identity is rooted in God's faithful love. God's love does not depend on what we do, but on who we are as children of God.

Pastor Leon has lost a clear sense of his importance in the eyes of God. His lack of self-care suggests that he is having trouble thinking highly enough of himself to take the time to be attentive to his own needs. He also feels discouraged and inadequate while attempting to keep up with demands at work and at home. This inadequacy pulls him into isolation from his colleagues and family and makes him more vulnerable to work-related and personal problems.

A Changing Family

What family issues are calling for Pastor Leon's attention? His family faces transition as a family unit. Pastor Leon struggles to know how to relate to his children, who are approaching adolescence. They remind him that he is getting older and he reviews this midpoint in life with some disappointment concerning his contentment at home and his productivity at work.

His growing children remind him that time is passing and neither his life nor his marriage is as fulfilling as it used to be. Leon's and Leah's marriage is changing, and they must find a way to grow as a couple. The family unit suffers from fragmentation, especially as the parents find it difficult to provide stability to their children while their marriage is vulnerable. The children react by acting out with poor grades, disciplinary problems, and low self-esteem due to the insecurity of their home environment. The children's symptoms demonstrate the imbalance of the whole family unit.

If Leon and Leah are to reconnect in a way that sustains their relationship and provides stability for their children, they will have to attend to a number of issues. One major issue, similar to what many ministers and families face, is how much time they spend together compared with how much time they spend apart at work and in individual time. Other issues include how Leon and Leah manage stress, resolve conflict, and regenerate warm feelings for one another. It will also be important for Leon to explore how the use of alcohol affects his life and relationship. The lack of collegial and extended family support are additional issues to address.

The Spirit Calls

Pastor Leon is being called by the Holy Spirit to make vocational choices that are life-affirming in the presence of difficult realities in Leesville. As the economy of the community declines, membership and financial giving decline as well. Leon needs to find ways to encourage his membership even though he himself feels personally discouraged. His own job security is directly affected, and the council has capped his salary for next year. He wonders how he can continue to be uplifting for his congregation while he himself feels psychologically down and spiritually depleted.

It is therefore all the more important for Leon to find a way to nurture himself so that he feels replenished enough to give to others. A vocational issue for Leon relates to his need for a healthy balance of work and time away. Currently, his work determines his life instead of him being in charge of his work schedule. While feeling overwhelmed he is less able to take control in decision-making, delegating tasks, and managing his time. As the feelings of being overwhelmed continue to increase, he is less likely to have energy to make choices to address his dilemma.

Leon's sense of helplessness makes him doubt that parish ministry is what he really wants to continue to do. He might not recognize this as a spiritual crisis, but his question about his vocation is a reflection of his wondering where God is in all of what he is experiencing right now. Did not God promise that the burden would be light (Matt. 11:30)? Where is God's care for the shepherd in ministry? Leon tries to put his troubling thoughts into prayer, but finds little energy to pray. He at times even wonders whether or not God is listening. Certainly, Leon is in need of hearing the good news of God's care and covenant promise.

THE COVENANT WITH ABRAHAM AND SARAH

God's selection of Abraham and Sarah to be bearers of the covenant (Gen. 12:1-3) follows a depressing story about how humanity was in a downward spiral that led to increasing levels of alienation from God. Alienation from the garden (3:22-24) led to alienation from one's very own ground (4:11-14) and eventually from the human community as the human family fragmented (11:8-9). In the midst of this hopeless state of total dissolution, Abraham and Sarah are chosen by God to renew the human community. As related in Israel's ancient epic tradition, God makes an unqualified commitment to grant Abraham and Sarah and their descendants a wonderful gift. The covenant is simple and direct: "When the sun had gone down and it was dark, a smoking fire pot and a flaming torch passed between these pieces. On that day the Lord made a covenant with Abram [and Sarah], saying, 'To your descendants I give this land, from the river of Egypt to the great river, the River Euphrates. . . .'" (Gen. 15:17-21). No ifs or buts, just an unconditional one-sided promise. Abraham and Sarah are simply to receive the gift.

Abraham and Sarah faced a major transition in leaving behind the familiarity of everything that they had previously known as they set out from Ur on the journey to Haran. Abraham and Sarah had no logical reason to believe that a land "flowing with milk and honey" would be theirs, much less theirs unconditionally. God's promise of descendants came to the elderly couple when conceiving, birthing, and rearing a child would seem impossible. In Genesis 15:5 we read, "God brought Abram outside and said, 'Look up at the sky and count the stars, if you can. So many will your descendants be.' Abram put his faith in the Lord, who reckoned it to him as righteousness." God is the one who provides in time of transition. And God provides when there seems to be no reason to hope.

The faith of Abraham and Sarah was lifted up as an example for the early church to follow. Hebrews 11 says that by faith Abraham (and Sarah) obeyed when called to set out for a place that (they) were to receive as an inheritance; and (they) set out, not knowing where (they) were going. By faith in God they received the promise of procreation, even though Abraham was too old—and Sarah herself was barren.

In the transition time of being homeless, uprooted, and unsure of what tomorrow would bring, Abraham and Sarah trusted in God to provide. And God's provision proved to be far beyond what the couple could have ever imagined.

Is there a way for us to hold on to the covenantal promise that God brings to us in times of transition? Can we recall the covenant that God made with Abraham and Sarah and let their faithful response inspire us to go forward in our daily life and ministries with hope?

Sometimes, in times of transition, God seems not to be present. Faith, "the substance of things hoped for, the evidence of things not seen" (Heb. 11:1), invites us in difficult times to recall the promise of Jesus: "I will not leave you desolate; I will come to you. Peace I leave with you; my peace I give to you; not as the world gives do I give to you. Let not your hearts be troubled, neither let them be afraid" (John 14:16b-19, 27).

The Holy Spirit intercedes for us when sighs are too deep for words at our most troubled times. God's Spirit is also alive in colleagues and supportive people in our lives who can bring a word of encouragement and hope to us when darkness comes.

GRACEFUL WAYS TO KEEP COVENANT IN TRANSITIONS

Two-by-Two

When did you last feel that you couldn't see the light at the end of the tunnel? Pastor Leon is feeling that way right now and his isolation makes his tunnel of troubles even darker and more difficult for him to see his way through. Many pastors in Leon's situation have found that what has helped them most during such times is regular, supportive contact with colleagues and friends.

Pastoral colleagues and colleague groups can provide support in a variety of ways. Leon needs a safe place where he can let down personally and not have to maintain his role as pastoral caregiver. A supportive group of colleagues can encourage him to take care of himself and share similar concerns, helping Leon not to feel so abnormal and alone. Many pastors have also found Bible study and prayer in a colleague group to be a time for spiritual renewal and helpful in replenishing energy for care giving. At this time when it is difficult for Leon to pray, a friend in a colleague group willing to pray for him or with him is a sign of God's presence and grace.

Colleagues can also serve as a sounding board to talk through situations that are stressful and problematic, such as Leon's confusion about the direction his relationship seems to be taking with Flo. Common challenges in working with church committees, councils, and situations in the parish can be shared among peers, leaving out the identifications of persons involved to protect confidentiality.[13] Such discussions can generate new ideas leading to greater optimism about finding a way to meet the challenges ministers face. Colleagues can offer the gift of affirmation, seeing strengths within us that we may overlook in ourselves during a down time.

Through this affirmation, we are encouraged to keep a more balanced picture of ourselves in ministry.

A trustworthy colleague may also provide Leon with an appropriate place for confidential sharing and self-disclosure. This could ease the burden that Leon carries and lessen the likelihood that he would start self-disclosure of very personal information to Flo, which would be inappropriate because she is a parishioner.

Developing solid relationships with colleagues who feel safe and provide for support in ministry takes time and intentional effort. Depending on our personality type and past experiences in reaching out and establishing such relationships, collegial relationships either come naturally or require more emotional risk. Colleague groups that are already established and defined around particular issues or purposes, such as pericope or book studies, may be more comfortable to join. Participation can be varied depending on comfort level. Sometimes just attending and listening to others can be helpful in working through our own situations.

Most important is to find a colleague or group of colleagues that can accept us and give us the message that we are good enough just as we are. To let go of always doing and performing in a role is to make steps toward self-nurturing in care of the caregiver.

We Have this Ministry

"Therefore, having this ministry by the grace of God, we do not lose heart" (2 Cor. 4:1). Paul sees God's grace as the source of our strength as ministers. To the early church in Corinth he writes: "Our competence is from God, who has made us competent to be ministers of a new covenant" (2 Cor. 3:5-6).

Paul also encourages the community at Ephesus to build up one another in love, practicing that which creates mutuality for the good of the community. While "speaking the truth in love," the body of Christ "joined and knit together by every joint with which it is supplied" can grow up in every way into Christ. With this mutual truth-telling, each part of the body works properly and the community grows and "upbuilds itself in love" (Eph. 4).

There are several forms or expressions of mutual ministry. When colleagues can comfortably approach one another with trust and reliability, a basis for mutuality is formed. If Leon were able to experience mutuality in a pastoral colleague group, it could help him work toward mutuality in ministry with members of his congregation.

Another expression of mutual ministry is found in staff ministries (more than one pastor, or several ministers on the same staff). An understanding of the personality type and leadership style of those with whom we work can enhance the mutuality of ministry. What time of day or evening is energy most available and productivity greatest for each individual staff member? Do staff members encourage one another to take adequate break times and days off? Are tasks scheduled and assignments delegated in a way that honors individual working styles and gifts for ministry?

Clear expectations, spoken and negotiated, can avoid misunderstandings that develop from misinformation at the start of a mutual relationship. Voicing disagreements when they first occur instead of allowing frustrations to build and become displaced and magnified also enhances working together.

It is especially challenging to build a mutual ministry when hierarchy is intrinsic to the roles and when there are titles like senior minister, associate pastor, and staff. To develop a team ministry that is truly mutual requires open communication, which is often helpfully facilitated by a consultant outside of the ministry team, perhaps someone available through the denominational office. The consultant can work with the team to see how members can support each other's strengths and best uplift each other's gifts. Ideas for how to establish the optimal working environment can be discussed. The consultant can guide the ministry team in formulating an approach to dealing with conflict as it arises.

A team of ministers can provide a model for how the congregation can work together for mutual ministry in the congregation. Each member of the congregation, being a steward of God's gifts, can then explore where he or she can best serve. Frederick Buechner writes on vocation in his book *Wishful Thinking: A Theological ABC:*

> The kind of work that God calls you to is the kind of work that
> (a) you need most to do and (b) that the world most needs to
> have done. . . . The place God calls you to is the place where
> your deep gladness and the world's deep hunger meet.[14]

Mutual ministry in the congregation can also be encouraged when the minister provides a model of self-care. Equipping leaders to notice signs of burnout is part of creating a mutual ministry style of congregational life. Volunteers will last longer in a task or activity that enables them to express their gifts. Encouraging members to take time to discover their gifts can facilitate good matching of the needs of ministry to those who would feel deep gladness serving in that particular area.

While speaking the truth in love, how can the congregation upbuild one another? Can members be encouraged to share the variety of gifts given by the one Spirit, as Paul describes in 1 Corinthians 12? The ministry staff can model for the congregation care for one another to encourage a community in which "if one member suffers, all suffer together; if one member is honored, all rejoice together."

According to John D. Vogelsang, a healthy congregation starts with a construct of justice, which includes the biblical concept of being in right relationship with each other. He explains, "A right relationship is one of mutual respect, empowerment, responsibility, trust, and choice." Concerning the nature of our behavior toward one another he states, "The question is not whether the act itself is wrong, but whether growth and integration are promoted, and the act is self-liberating, other enhancing, honest, faithful, socially responsible, life-serving, and joyous."[15]

Vogelsang talks about the characteristics of a healthy congregation such as a clear sense of mission, mutual responsibility and accountability, a clear sense of boundaries, dynamic worship and networks of listening, connection, and appreciation. A healthy congregation supports healthy and just relationships so that mutual ministry can happen for the good of the whole church in the world in our stewardship of God's creation.

Ministers and members of congregations can provide for an experience of mutual ministry as together they proclaim the gospel of Jesus Christ. Mutuality is encouraged when we give of ourselves for another as Christ gave himself for us.

Many pastors have found pastor-parish committees or mutual ministry committees to be very helpful in creating a climate of mutual ministry in the congregation. In *Mutual Ministry Committee: A Vision for Building Up the Body of Christ*, George Keck states that the gospel is entrusted by God to us as earthen vessels. We can both empty ourselves "for" others and can be filled "from" others in a mutual way. "Without this mutual ministry our earthen vessels will soon be empty and have no ministry for the world."[16] Who cares for the caregiver? Day after day, Pastor Leon is expected to care for others in preaching, teaching, listening, visiting, and planning. Like all ministers, he empties himself for the sake of the gospel. And, like all ministers, there comes a time when he needs to be filled or cared "for," too.

How can a mutual ministry committee equip and support ministers so they can be the best servants to the congregation? Central to mutual ministry is a theology of the priesthood of all believers where all the baptized are called to be engaged in the mission of the church. The mutual ministry committee can support the ministry of the congregation through careful listening, reflecting, caring and praying for the staff. The committee members serve as advocates for the staff in times of personal or professional stress and in times of congregational crisis or conflict. They are a listening post for the staff and speak together candidly about ministerial concerns while working together to encourage healthy communication in the congregation. The committee also supports ministers in planning for their continuing education and in taking time off and making time for family. Pastor Leon does not have such a committee in his congregation. If he had, Leon might be experiencing less of a sense of isolation at this time and more of a sense of support.

A Cloud of Witnesses

> Through toil and tribulation
> And tumult of her war,
> She waits the consummation
> Of peace for evermore;
> Till with the vision glorious
> Her longing eyes are blest,
> And the great Church victorious
> Shall be the Church at rest.
> "The Church's One Foundation"[17]

Throughout history the church has faced distress and disaster, problems and persecution. Saints, their watch keeping, have cried, "How long, O Lord?" And yet the church survives and even thrives, finding her way through the struggle by the grace of God. Until we see God face to face when our rest is won, the challenges continue. Strength for the journey can be found in knowing that there are saints who have gone before us.

Have you ever felt the presence of a cloud of witnesses cheering you on? Hebrews 12:1ff. states, "Therefore, since we are surrounded by so great a cloud of witnesses, let us also lay aside every weight and the sin that clings so closely, and let us run with perseverance the race that is set before us, looking to Jesus the pioneer and perfecter of our faith." Do you remember people of the faith who inspired you to continue the race with perseverance? What about the first person who told you the good news of God's love in Jesus Christ and encouraged you in your faith? Living saints and the saints of God's heavenly Kingdom surround us. What confidence and assurance we receive from God's promise of the Spirit's presence through these members of the body of Christ!

The church is ever changing and growing over time. Like any system, the church is always in transition and fluid in structure. The church must be open to change to be the presence of Christ alive in the world. Seeing this larger picture can be beneficial for a leader in times of transition. For Leon, reviewing the history of the Leesville church even prior to his becoming the pastor can help him see the characteristic patterns of interaction that have surfaced in the Leesville congregation during other times of crisis. Also, reading books like Edwin Friedman's *Generation to Generation* and Peter Steinke's *How Your Church Family Works* helps identify dynamics that could affect any congregation.[18] How could this knowledge help Leon feel less personally responsible for reactions and conflicts in the congregation? How can knowing that God in Jesus shares our struggle in this race that is set before us sustain Leon in the days ahead? How can the mystic sweet communion we share with our Lord nourish us for the mission of the church? The truth that the church's one foundation is Jesus Christ our Lord empowers us for ministry!

Pastoral colleague groups, mutual ministry support committees, and a sense of the church over recent history and over all of Christian history could bring additional perspective into Leon's ministry in Leesville. But Leon at the moment has none of these benefits. It may take time to find a group or form a committee in which he can place his trust. The most immediate step he can take is to come to terms with the dilemma of self-care.

3

COVENANT & SELF-CARE

THE SELF-CARE DILEMMA
Whose Need?

Pastor Leon is in a dilemma right now. Vocationally, interpersonally in his family, and personally he is at a choice-point. The congregation is showing signs of decline, both in number of members and in finances. While there are increasing needs and demands from congregants, Pastor Leon is feeling less support. At home, Leon's relationship with his wife and children is at a low ebb. He still misses what was, which is a sign that he remembers and cares, but he hates the hassle of rehashing his shortcomings with Leah and finds it easier simply to avoid confrontation by withdrawing. Personally, he is vulnerable to crossing an ethical boundary with his parishoner, Flo.

Leon's situation illustrates the self-care dilemma. In the midst of so many demands and the temptation to meet personal needs, what is appropriate self-care? Are there any principles that can guide a minister as that minister makes choices between providing ministry to others and nurturing oneself?

A career counselor once spoke about two of the scales of an instrument that has been used to discern who would make a good candidate for ministry. One scale was used to identify how much the candidate was oriented toward caring for others. The second scale was used to identify how much the candidate was oriented toward caring for self. The theory was that ministers, and others in helping vocations, should be more concerned about caring for others than for self, so if the second scale (care of self) was considerably elevated and especially if it were higher than the first scale (care of others), there were questions about that person's motivation for ministry. Was the person interested in caring for God's people or more interested in being taken care of? On the other hand, it is also possible for a minister to be so oriented toward taking care of others that it is almost impossible to say "no" even when it would be more faithful to do so.

There are those who oppose any kind of personality testing in discerning whether or not a person is an appropriate candidate for ministry. Some oppose such methods because the call of God to ministry is the work of the Holy Spirit. The concern is that a test result may lead those who make such decisions to say "no" when the Holy Spirit is saying "yes."

A person is always more than a test result, no matter how sophisticated the test. Therefore, those who use testing in the ministerial candidacy process always should do so with care and in combination with other ways of getting to know a person, such as personal interviews. Testing can be helpful if it is perceived not as a final answer to the question of appropriateness for ministry, but as a way of helping to identify the areas of personal thought, feeling, and behavior that need to be explored more fully in personal interviews with the candidate. From that perspective, when self-care is elevated higher than other care, it could be useful to discuss sample pastoral care situations where there is a need both for ministry to others and for self-care. In the interview, how the candidate proposes balancing self-care and other care needs would help to interpret what the elevations on the test scales could be reflecting.

If Pastor Leon were in a denomination that provided pastoral consultation to pastors, he might at this point in his ministry benefit from taking advantage of such a consultation.[19] There are those who are skilled in making pastoral assessments when ministers are at choice-points in their vocation or in their family or personal life. If such a consultation is not readily available, sometimes a ministry colleague or another professional or a wise, reasonably objective and trusted friend can help us as ministers deal with the self-care dilemma.

When it comes to ministry with congregants, it is always helpful to ask ourselves the question that a seminary professor, David Ostergren, always wrote on the chalkboard when asked a pastoral care question that required a balance of care for others and care for self.[20] He wrote only two words, but there was a world of meaning behind them: *"Whose Need?"* Dr. Ostergren's consistent message was that in pastoral ministry the need we are to be responding to is not our own need but that of the one we are serving. For Dr. Ostergren, the self-care dilemma was real, but the way to resolve it was to minister in the parish and to meet personal needs outside the congregation.

Dr. Ostergren would encourage Pastor Leon not to reduce his personal world to the congregation in Leesville, because if he does he will look to the congregation not only as the place where he serves others but as the only place where he can get his own needs met. To see one's place of service as also the primary place where one is served puts a minister at high risk for crossing boundaries.

Before we look at how Pastor Leon resolves his personal self-care dilemma, it is important that we recognize that all ministers face this dilemma. Then, too, some ministers, like his friend Pastor María, have additional challenges.

Special Challenges in Ministry

Women in Ministry. Pastor María faces particular challenges as a single parent and a woman in ministry. She is challenged to manage family needs while taking care of church needs, and she has learned that care for herself is crucial in order to meet the challenge. The need for a support network of female and male colleagues has proved helpful for her to talk over issues related to stress, self-care, and vocation. She has appreciated the insights gained in dialogue with her male pastoral colleagues, especially in the area of appropriate professional boundaries in ministry.

Being in a traditional male role as a pastor, María has also found the feminine voice of peers especially supportive in the areas of assertiveness and pastoral identity. Clergywomen often face the difficulty of being comfortable with their own power and authority. A challenge is to not suppress their gifts and leadership in the midst of a male message to do so. In a patriarchal world, society, and church in which colleagues, politicians, government officers, senior pastors, deans, CEOs, judges, and bishops are predominantly men, finding one's feminine voice is often hard.

María recalls the contrast of two experiences at church gatherings. One was while she was singing hymns at a church assembly with area pastors. She sang with all the voice she had and was still unable to hear herself or any other woman because of the deep male voices that drowned out the female voices. It was like drowning out her soul.

The second experience was singing at an anniversary celebration of the ordination of women, where for the first time in fifteen years of attending church assemblies she heard the sound of women filling the room. Also for the first time she sensed a clergy identity beyond herself, a collective that she actually felt she belonged to. With this experience she felt strengthened to voice her ideas and claim her gifts within the existing structures of the church.

Carol Gilligan explores psychological theory and women's development in her book *In a Different Voice.*[21] In a society in which male experience is the norm, Gilligan calls for theories of psychological development derived from feminine experience. Gilligan challenges the assumption that male-based theories apply equally to women. She believes by bringing women's voices into the open we engage in an ongoing process of changing the voice of the world.

Rosemary Radford Ruether celebrates women's spirituality in *Women-Church* and offers rites of passage and rituals for community that respect and nurture the feminine experience.[22] Writers like Carol Gilligan and Ruether increase awareness of the way a patriarchal system can suppress feminine wisdom and how spiritual growth is enhanced for both women and men when the feminine voice is truly heard.

For María, gathering with other women provides an arena for her to explore who she is and her role as a professional, woman, mother, grandmother, and friend. In such a supportive group, María can learn new ways to affirm herself in the midst of marginalization, to conceive of herself as powerful as she honors her gentle leadership style, and to be vocal about her needs in ecclesiastical circles. In a support group, María is encouraged to grow in her skills and dedication as a pastor, and to serve as a mentor for other women in ministerial roles. She is strengthened in her ministry to people in the parish. Because she is uplifted by the voices of her sisters, her own voice is stronger and clearer for the sake of ministry. To gather together to pray and sing with other women is a way to cultivate her own gifts and to be strengthened for her ministry both with women and with men.

Singles in Ministry. Being single, María faces additional challenges in ministry. Parishioners may perceive the single minister to be more available to parish needs and better able to manage more work responsibilities because of the assumption single ministers have more time to devote to the church. They also may be seen as more open to drop-ins at home. Privacy may be more difficult to maintain.

For self-care, the single pastor, like everyone, needs connections with others. Where does the single pastor go to be replenished and renewed? María is to be there for her parishioners, to meet their needs. Because it is inappropriate to expect parishioners to meet her personal needs, it is important that she have colleagues and friends outside the church. The challenge is how to manage this self-care with clear boundaries.

For example, the single minister may experience loneliness at family potlucks and other gatherings or receptions when families are invited. Does the single minister attend alone, or bring a friend or a date and then face awkwardness as others romanticize or comment about the relationship? The congregation may take pleasure or even feel responsible for fixing up the single minister with a parishioner. It is, however, a boundary challenge, because dating a parishioner presents a dual relationship. The dual roles of minister and dating partner create an ethical bind for a professional. If the relationship does not work out, not only is the dating relationship lost but the ministerial relationship would be affected. Ethically, dual relationships with parishoners are to be avoided because of the potential for the misuse of power and authority inherent in the role of the minister.[23]

Single ministers may find that their denomination or judicatory has helpful guidelines for ethical relationships with parishioners and appropriate dating relationships outside the congregation. Sometimes a pastoral colleague group that meets regularly is a context in which potentially sticky situations can be checked out in advance, before boundaries are crossed and harm results. Most importantly, along with all ministers, a single minister like María will want to safeguard the integrity of her ministry. Anticipating potential problems and thinking through faithful ways to avoid them is wiser than to wait until an uncomfortable situation develops where a parishioner could be hurt and a ministry jeopardized.

Multicultural Ministry. Pastor María brings to ministry a rich heritage. Her mother is an Anglo and her father is Hispanic. The Germanic background of her mother instilled in María a strong work ethic and a desire for order and organization. She learned from her mother not to show her inner feelings in public. On the other hand, her father was outwardly very warm and emotionally expressive. Her father would make a fuss over her and her siblings and showered them with praise. He would hug people he met for the first time, even other men, as physical expressions of greeting were culturally appropriate. He taught María respect for elders and a strong identification with family. Loyalty and courage and respect for authority were virtues María saw in her father, and which she internalized in herself.[24]

María is the first multicultural minister to serve her congregation. She is also the first woman minister and the first single pastor. Not only does María struggle with questions of pastoral identity but her presence also challenges the congregation to expand their vision of ministers and ministry. Even if she were not relatively new to ministry, the integration of all the facets of her personal background with the professional firsts would be enough to challenge anyone. In the past, most of the members of her Leesville congregation were Anglo, although the neighborhood immediately around the church was beginning to change. If her presence attracts persons of other cultures to her congregation, she will also face the possibility of reaction from a number of the older members, some of whom want the congregation to remain the same. A few of them were also opposed to María's being called as the pastor, perhaps because they foresaw change if she were invited to come.

Being female, single, and of a minority culture in the community brings with it a particular challenge in ministry. If there can be an appreciation for diversity within the church as well as a commitment to unity in Christ, then the kinds of differences personified in María can contribute to the richness that God intends in calling to ministry those with differing gifts. At the same time, it will likely be stressful for María until she is seen by the congregation not simply as different, but as the gifted person that she is.

Great Expectations

Another challenge to ministry comes from something that is often not explicit, but nevertheless always present: expectations. Earlier we cited

David Goetz's survey of 748 pastors in which Goetz found that 63 percent identified congregational expectations as part of the problem ministers face. Expectations were also prominent problems in the research results of Donald Houts, Stephen Daniel, and Martha Rogers.[25] Daniel and Rogers reviewed the literature about burnout and found many of the variables "include stress from constant interpersonal contact and continually increasing effort to meet the rigorous demands and expectations."[26]

We also noted earlier that the common thread Craig Ellison and William Mattila saw running through each of the most pressing problems ministers experience had to do with expectations: "unrealistic expectations promote constant time demands. . . . It appears that frustration, depression, and feelings of inadequacy . . . are also produced in part by the failure to meet expectations. . . ." Therefore, it seemed to them, "that idealism and high expectations are a common base for the most frequently indicated problems, often due to a perceived gap between what is desired and what is achieved in the specific context of ministry."[27]

From the standpoint of appropriate self-care, it is vital that the minister realize that the expectations that so often lead to distress do not just come from the congregation. When the minister misperceives the congregation as the problem, then the problem is out there and those out there (antagonistic lay leader, difficult coworker or staff member, resistant council or board, unsupportive members, etc.) are to blame for how the minister feels. Posing the problem as due to the expectations of others can lead a minister to feel helpless ever to be able to meet those expectations, especially since some of those expectations are clearly contradictory and meeting the expectations of some inevitably means not meeting the expectations of those who have opposite expectations.

Expectations from a congregation are real and must be dealt with in a realistic and pastoral way. However, the research suggests that much of what leads ministers to "frustration, depression, and feelings of inadequacy" are the idealistic expectations we lay on ourselves. If, in the face of contradictory expectations on the part of parishioners, we also expect ourselves somehow to meet those contradictory expectations, we set ourselves up for failure. Even if congregational expectations are not contradictory, but simply very high, we can also set ourselves up for failure if we think that there is only one way to meet those expectations—with a 25-hour day. Expecting ourselves to be all things for all people not only misreads the Pauline Epistles but also makes it less likely that the gifts for service that God distributes throughout the members of the congregation will ever be called forth into service. Faithful ministry brings forth and upbuilds the gifts of others.

In short, our own expectations about meeting expectations can be an even larger part of the problem than the expectations laid on ministers by others. To recognize this does not just add one more responsibility on us; it actually makes it possible for us to do something about our dilemma of self-care. If we see our problems as out there, there is relatively little we can do about our situation unless someone out there changes. On the other hand, if we see that a good deal of the problem lies not out there, but in here, with ourselves, then we can go about the process of changing the only person we ever really can change—ourselves.

Change, however, takes courage. Are there ways in which covenant is linked not only with care, but with the encouragement we need to consider changing anything that needs to be changed? To answer that question, not only the covenant with Abraham and Sarah, but also God's covenant with Moses can be helpful.

THE COVENANT WITH MOSES

What can we learn about change from covenant theology? Quite distinct from the idea of the covenant made with Abraham and Sarah, there is a later tradition that speaks of a covenant made with Moses on Mount Sinai, a covenant marked by an actual treaty document—the two tablets of stone—which was kept in the ark of the covenant. What characterized this covenant tradition, unlike the earlier one between Yahweh and Abraham and Sarah, was the fact that there was a list of conditions attached to this treaty. Indeed the commandments inscribed on the stone tablets were only representative of a much larger body of conditions or laws (Torah) that were given to instruct Israel in its daily life, laws that would set it apart from communities around it. A continuing relationship with God could be impaired or derailed depending upon how faithfully Israel kept Torah.

Furthermore, the promise given with this treaty did not relate specifically to the *gift of land* itself but more to the *gift of relationship with God* in the land. It was a covenant marked by ambiguity and threat, a two-edged sword that offered not only a way of life but also a way of death. Moses' successor, Joshua, would eventually proclaim in a voice already recognizing the course of history that Israel was fundamentally incapable of keeping this covenant faithfully (Josh. 24:19-23).[28]

What the covenant with Moses suggests is that our actions do make a difference to God and the life of the community of faith. The new covenant through Christ Jesus does not minimize the importance of faithful actions as an expression of our love for God. Faith leading to works, faith in action, is very consistent with the gospel.[29] The difference that the gospel (good news) makes is that we do not go about our good works as if our life and salvation depend on what we do, because of what God already has done for us in Christ Jesus. The Mosaic law is not the way of life, and salvation does not come from following the law. The gospel is that Christ is "the way, and the truth, and the life" (John 14:6) and salvation comes as a free gift from God. Because God gracefully accepts us through our Lord and Savior and because such love is given to us not through our own good deeds but as a gift, we show our thanksgiving with the way we live our life.

Choosing, then, to change those things in ourselves that we need to change is an expression of our gratitude to God. We are free to change because we do not have to change to be acceptable to God. That is good news. It also is a motivating word, because unconditional love has a way of inspiring us to respond in loving ways.

If Pastor Leon or Pastor María wanted to change some things in their lives, what would be helpful for them to keep in mind as they make and keep a self-care covenant?

GRACEFUL WAYS TO KEEP A SELF-CARE COVENANT

Wholeness in the Bible

Faithful self-care calls us to remember that God has created us as whole people. Therefore, holistic self-care requires that we pay attention to three personal dimensions of wholeness: the physical, the mental, and the emotional.

Physical Self-Care. In the Old Testament, when the Hebrews thought of the body they did not think of it as simply something a person has, as in, "I have a body and it is sore from working in the vineyards too long." Hebrew thinking is more boldly stated in the following way: "The Hebrew idea of the personality is an animated body . . . (A person) does not *have* a body, (the person) *is* a body."[30]

One of the changes that Pastor Leon needs to make is his care of his body. He is experiencing physical symptoms of distress. Dismissing chest pain as simply stress, relieved by drinking alcohol, is not faithful self-care. Not only could there be underlying heart disease but also the potential for dependency on the chemical alcohol (or any other chemical) is increased by its use for stress reduction. If a person is prone to physical addiction, becoming dependent on chemicals to relieve stress can lead to addiction.

A step toward more faithful physical self-care would be for Leon to see his family physician or a recommended specialist so he could check out his physical symptoms. The physician would also need to know Leon's current ways of coping with these symptoms. Leon's use of alcohol should not be kept secret from the physician, for faithful self-care requires complete honesty when seeking help from a professional.

The change in patterns of physical intimacy with his spouse would also be relevant, as there are a number of reasons why a person may lose sexual desire. When there are interpersonal conflicts, it is easy to assume that the reason for these changes is known, but sometimes the symptom is more complicated than it appears. The loss of sexual interest can also be a sign of depression.

Mental Self-Care. The Book of Proverbs says that as a person thinks, so is that person (23:7). This, of course, does not mean that any random thoughts that flit through our minds define us as a people, but it does suggest that those thoughts that we dwell upon indicate something about who we are. Martin Luther is reported to have said that you cannot keep the birds from flying over your head, but you can stop them from building a nest there!

The field of cognitive-behavioral psychology is gaining prominence in our psychosocial self-understanding. A key component of the cognitive-behavioral approach is that how we perceive ourselves and our life situations has a great deal to do with how we respond. If we view ourselves as helpless and hopeless, we are more likely to perceive a challenging situation as a threat rather than as an opportunity.

Faithful mental self-care for Leon could involve his making an appointment with a pastoral counselor or a community psychiatrist, psychologist, or other local counselor to check out how he is perceiving his situation. He might find that there are alternatives to his way of looking at things that he has not even considered. When we are personally involved in a situation, it is very difficult to look at that situation with complete objectivity. Someone who is outside our situation can often help us see things that we would otherwise unintentionally overlook.

Emotional Self-Care. The Psalms are a primary resource for us as persons gifted by God with the capacity for feeling. The range of emotions expressed through the Psalms covers the heights of praise and joy with the depths of despair and lament. Many other places in the Bible suggest that it is faithful to have feelings and to express them to the Lord, but the Psalms in a special way give most persons the very words that most closely fit their emotional needs.

Faithful emotional self-care requires a context of nonjudgmental acceptance with someone who will listen and explore feelings rather than someone who wants prematurely to close them off or say something like, "You shouldn't feel that way." For ministers, it is questionable judgment to use a member of the congregation for this kind of listening, because it is the minister's calling and role to be there as this kind of listener when the *parishioner* has feelings that need to be ventilated. When the minister is the one ventilating feelings, the minister may say something that would cause the parishioner to want to take care of the minister and not add to the minister's burdens by seeking pastoral care, even when the parishioner needs care. In effect, parishioners who are used by ministers to meet the minister's needs may end up feeling like they have no pastor. For emotional self-care and care taking, the minister wisely seeks out not someone the minister is to be serving, but rather a pastoral colleague who is able and willing to listen in an accepting way, or a counselor (psychologist, psychiatrist, pastoral counselor, or other) who can hear without responding with judgment.

Having feelings is not the same as acting on them. Feelings are neither right nor wrong, good nor bad. What we do with our feelings—how we choose to act on them—can be appropriate or inappropriate. A trained counselor can help us sort out our sometimes conflicting feelings and guide us in the ways to express or act on those feelings that are consistent with our values and responsibilities. Leon has a lot of ambivalent feelings right now—personally, interpersonally, and vocationally. Faithful emotional self-care would be a lot more likely if he were consulting with a counselor during this difficult time in his life and ministry.

Asking the God-Question

Not only is Pastor Leon stressed about his congregation and his home life situation, but he is also wrestling with spiritual issues when he is trying to figure out what to do. In the words of CPE Chaplain Carl Nighswonger, there is a God-question at the heart of every troubling situation.[31] While Pastor Leon undoubtedly preaches to others about how God is actively involved not only on Sunday but also during the week, he may or may not recognize the spiritual nature of his own struggle at this time. The Bible tells us that when we face perplexing life problems they engage us as whole persons. The physical, mental, and emotional dimensions of personhood are interrelated and interactive. What affects one part does not just affect that part, because biblically we are not made up of parts. When in one of the Psalms David asks that God create in him a clean heart, he is talking about being renewed as a whole person (Ps. 51:20).[32]

Each significant situation not only shows us how interrelated and interactive the dimensions of our humanness are, but also raises a God-question. This God-question can help us grow spiritually or can give us insight into areas of potential spiritual growth for us personally, since God-questions are at the core of who we are as people of God.

In chapter 5 we shall have an opportunity to look more deeply into spirituality and the God-questions implicit in Leon's situation. For now, however, we focus on the three personal dimensions: physical, mental, and emotional.

A Personal Covenant

Leon would benefit from making a covenant of personal self-care. If a person wanted to make a covenant that embraced the physical, mental, and emotional dimensions of our lives, it would be helpful to take a look at some of the things that could facilitate or interfere with keeping such a covenant. Whether you are working through this book on your own or with a study group, take a few minutes now to ask yourself the following questions:

Personal Covenant

In my family of origin, *what did I learn about rest and relaxation, nutrition, physical activity? What did I learn about education—its place and importance? Were my accomplishments acknowledged and praised? Growing up, what made me feel most appreciated? Most intellectually competent? Most intellectually inadequate? Were emotions expressed? If so, how? Were feelings respected?*

Now, as an adult, *what do I recognize in my present life that reflects my experiences growing up in my family? How has my experience in ministry reinforced my early learnings?*

Do I have someone (a professional or a friend or a colleague) with whom I can discuss my personal history? What difference does it make that I do or that I don't? If I don't have someone else to talk with, would it be helpful to establish such a relationship as part of a covenant I make with myself?

My covenant in this personal area which could lead to my growth as an embodied, thinking, feeling person in Christ:

4

COVENANT & FAMILY

ALL IN THE FAMILY
A Balancing Act

How can Pastor Leon balance his own needs with those of his family and the Leesville congregation? At this point we find Leon feeling inadequate in all areas of his life. Is it possible for him to regain a sense of having choices so that he doesn't feel as helpless and overwhelmed?

Pastor María faces similar challenges. She shares Leon's frustration with finding time for herself. She has been wanting to take a yoga class with a friend for some months but has no evenings free. She barely has enough time to do household chores, even less to respond to the needs of her family and friends. Involvement with her children and grandchildren are important to her. How can María balance her roles as mother, grandmother, pastor, and friend in a way that feels more healthy to her?

FIRST THINGS FIRST

Both Leon and María find the demands at work to be never ending. One occupational hazard in the ministry is the potential to overwork due to the ambiguous boundaries of the job. How can one avoid not taking work home when the phone rings with one request after another to talk just for a minute or when Sunday's sermon weighs heavily on the heart? How can ministers structure the tasks of ministry to feel a sense of accomplishment for a day's work when there are always so many tasks left undone?

Another balancing act involves administrative versus other pastoral responsibilities. How can the pastor be a full-time administrator in the office and an on-call, twenty-four-hour-a-day caregiver and do both jobs well? Pastor Leon finds office work frustrating after the church administrative assistant was let go due to financial pressures, and he has only periodic volunteer help. Even with hired help, there were complications. Leon, like many ministers, had a church member as an employee. When staff are also parishioners and when staff persons are in personal need the well-being of the parishoner is primary. Even if the parishioner-staff person has no particular personal needs, energy and time are still required to maintain healthy relationships among the office staff through good communication skills and clear boundaries.

THE WAY WE WERE

A relevant question for ministers is: How did the skills they learned growing up in their family of origin equip them for the challenges of ministry? Did Leon experience a sense of confidence in his relationships with his family members? Were his talents identified and embraced and celebrated? Or was he unsure whether or not he had important gifts to offer others because they were overlooked by his parents or key adult figures?

We carry what we learned in our family of origin into our ministry style. What did we learn about the meaning of commitment, the decision-making process, the expression or nonexpression of emotion? How did we manage conflict in our families? The ways we learned to handle or avoid conflict will carry over into the parish. Are we able to see conflict and maintain objectivity, or do we tend to be affected by conflict to the point where we act out in frustration or freeze in fear, not knowing how to respond?

Out of pain can also grow the gift of ministry. Our sensitivity to pain can help us respond when we see someone else in need. How can strength develop out of adversity? Strength for later ministry comes from growing through problems, rather than denying them or avoiding the discomfort of difficult times. For the sake of ministry, it is important to face our demons and dragons within, to face the wounds we carry from our family of origin and growing-up experiences so that we can find healing and also learn from the pain.

In theological language this is living out a theology of the cross. In the cross, God identifies with our pain. God in Christ experienced human suffering and knows what it is like to feel abandonment, physical and emotional distress, and alienation. God is present with us when we hurt.

Ministers from biblical times on have grown through pain. The apostle Paul had a thorn in the flesh and also endured shipwrecks, beatings, and stoning, yet could write: "More than that, we rejoice in our sufferings, knowing that suffering produces endurance, and endurance produces character, and character produces hope, and hope does not disappoint us, because God's love has been poured into our hearts through the Holy Spirit which has been given to us (Rom. 5:3-5).

How can Pastor Leon and other ministers receive the transforming power of God's love, which embraces our pain and finds ways of healing—not around the pain but through it? In our baptism into Christ we identify with Christ in death, but also in new life. Is there a way to find joy in the midst of pain? Can we, through our own suffering, find additional ways to be empathic and to be present for others? Can we use our painful experiences to develop the compassion necessary for healthy care of self, healthy relationships with friends and family, and healthy ministry in the congregation? In what ways would Leon's recalling a sense of God's love and covenantal faithfulness strengthen him for his pastoral ministry to others?

THE COVENANT THROUGH GENERATIONS

> I will sing of your steadfast love, O LORD, for ever;
> with my mouth I will proclaim
> your faithfulness to all generations.
> I declare that your steadfast love is
> established forever;
> your faithfulness is as firm as the heavens.
> You said, "I have made a covenant
> with my chosen one,
> have sworn to my servant David:
> 'I will establish your descendants forever,
> and build your throne for all generations.'"
> —Psalm 89:1-4

The language of Psalm 89 boldly speaks of God's covenant made with David, "God's chosen one," God's "firstborn" whose line shall be established forever, as sure as are the foundations of the earth themselves (cf. Ps. 132:12). The language of this covenant is much like that of the Deuteronomic language of worship reflecting God's presence in the life of the community. The covenant connects generation to generation in a life-giving force within the community of God's people.[33]

God's covenant throughout generations reveals God's intention to be with humanity through the ages. What strength for the healing journey can be received from such a commitment by God to humankind? In the person of Mary, God again promises that generation after generation will know God's love through the child Jesus. In the great *Magnificat* Mary sings, "My soul magnifies the Lord, and my spirit rejoices in God my savior . . . surely from now on all generations will call me blessed" (Luke 1:46ff.). Mary, blessed among women, gives birth to Jesus who will fill the hungry with good things. The God of Israel had mercy on Abraham and Sarah, Isaac and Rebekah, Jacob and Rachel, and all generations that followed, through David, and now through Jesus, God continues to speak a covenantal word of love.

In Psalm 100 we see that God's steadfast love and faithfulness to all generations is connected to creation. In verse 3 the psalmist writes, "Know that the LORD is God. It is God that made us, and we are God's; we are God's people, and the sheep of God's pasture." Because we are eternally held by God as God's children, we can go about the shepherding task of ministry, which is to hold others in God's loving care. It is as if God encircles us with compassion as a community while we show compassion to one another. It is indeed God's embrace of us that empowers our embracing of others!

GRACEFUL WAYS TO KEEP COVENANT WITH FAMILY

Becoming a Person

A holistic model of personhood does not treat the physical, mental, and emotional dimensions of humanness as unrelated, but rather as interactive with each other. What significantly affects a person in any one dimension will affect that person in the other dimensions as well. For example, a headache will not only affect the body, but also our concentration and our ability to be emotionally available to someone who wants to talk with us while our head is pounding.

In addition to the dimensions of humanness and their interrelatedness and interaction, there is also another dynamic that is part of each of us: the dynamic of an individual's personal history. What has happened to us in the course of our lifetimes as embodied, thinking, and feeling persons also affects our senses of who we are. Personal identity ties our past into the present. Our past and present are so interwoven that one could even say, "I am my history."

One way to understand how our personal histories are linked to our present identities is through the study of human development and the life cycle. In *Pastor as Person*, the work of Erik Erikson is presented as one of the most helpful developmental theories for a minister's self-understanding and for ministry to others.[34] Erikson discusses the entire life cycle from birth to death. He is concerned for not only the psychological, but also for the biological, the social, and the cultural facets of human development. For Erikson the early years of a person's life are critical but do not completely determine the course of later life. At each of the eight stages of life he sees the individual faced with a developmental crisis that builds on the past and prepares the person for the next stage or task of healthy development.

In many ways we are our histories, but it is also important to remind ourselves that we are *more* than our histories. As we discussed earlier, God can transform even the most painful experiences of our past, and we can move beyond past beliefs, behaviors, or traumas toward greater health. At the same time, being familiar with our developmental past and what is still unresolved will assist us in taking care of ourselves and those with whom we live, work, and play. Also, in knowing our own histories we can all the more appreciate how the histories of others have been a shaping force for them, too.

Erikson says that in the first year of life the task is to gain a healthy balance of trust over mistrust. For future growth the child must learn from the mother figure that the world can be approached in a trusting way. There can be too much as well as too little mothering, so human development is more complex than simply whether or not our needs were met and how we responded. Erikson suggests that how confident ministers or other individuals are that their needs will be met, or even be of interest to the world (environment, family, the congregation, God), is related to, though not completely determined by, this earliest stage of human development.

During the next stage the critical task, according to Erikson, is to come out of the second year of life with more autonomy than shame and self-doubt. The child begins to sense that he or she is not identical with the care-taker/parent and declares that autonomy with the first uses of the word "no." While issues of dependency highlight the first stage of development, in the second stage control issues are more important. If ministers and other people have unresolved struggles in the area of autonomy and control, this may contribute to their being sensitive to authority or other powerful figures and to how they feel about and exercise the right to be themselves.

During the remainder of the preschool years, we had the task of developing our dependence and independence in relation to others by learning to take initiative without feeling guilt. Continuing on in development in the early school years the task is to overcome feelings of inferiority so we are able to do and perform. We can see how unresolved issues in these areas would prove challenging to the interpersonal functioning of a minister.

According to Erikson, the adolescent is faced with the task of establishing an identity while also contending with painful self-doubt and the biological changes of puberty. In young adulthood, the individual's task is to resolve questions of intimacy versus isolation. True intimacy is possible only when two persons with relatively stable identities choose to be together. A minister who carries unresolved conflict concerning self-esteem and self-identity may find it difficult to maintain an appropriate balance of separateness and connectedness with parishioners, and may also be more vulnerable to conflict in the parish.

Generativity and Integrity mark the last two stages of Erikson's theory of development. Generativity means concern for others in a creative and caring way. Ministry requires meeting the needs of others for nurture. Potential problems arise when the minister's need *to* nurture is confused with the need *for* nurture. The successful management of this phase of life is important to move into the final stage of development, the stage of Integrity. Values of fidelity, care, wisdom, and hope are identified as important in this final stage. Erikson says experiencing life as an integrated whole in this stage makes it possible to see death without despair.

Erikson's stages of development, like many traditional studies, seem to reflect the male more than the female experience. Lyn Mikel Brown, Annie Rogers, Carol Gilligan, and other members of the Harvard Project on Women's Psychology and the Development of Girls are giving voice to girls' experience. In *Women's Ways of Knowing: The Development of Self, Voice, and Mind*, authors Mary Field Belenky, Blithe McVicker Clinchy, Nancy Rule Goldberger, and Jill Mattuck Tarule weave the feminine experience with theology and psychotherapy.[35]

Carol Gilligan, in her book *In a Different Voice*, encourages further research on development that describes "in women's own terms the experience of their adult life."[36] Gilligan explains that there are differences between males and females around experiences of attachment and separation. While autonomy is highly valued in the male experience, connection or attachment is most valued in the female experience. Life transitions reflect a woman's sense of integrity that is "intertwined with an ethic of care, so that to see themselves in a relationship as women is to see themselves in a relationship of connection." Gilligan believes that tasks in life transitions are to be centered around the redefinition of care. She states, "When the distinction between helping and pleasing frees the activity of taking care from the wish for approval by others, the ethic of responsibility can become a self-chosen anchor of personal integrity and strength."

Working with the System

In addition to theories of human development and the life cycle, how could an understanding of family systems theory assist the minister in strengthening covenant relationships with self, family, and others? Along with the expertise of Erik Erikson and Carol Gilligan, the work of Murray Bowen, a founder of family systems theory, can contribute to understanding individuals in relationship to their environments and communities.[37]

Pastor Leon's family can be seen as a family system of individuals who are interconnected to one another in such a way that the actions of one family member affects the whole family. Leon, Leah, Leo, and Lisa interact and function interdependently. Change in one person affects the whole family. The family also interacts with their environment in terms of communication with church, school, Leah's workplace, and the neighborhood. In turn, what happens in their environment affects the family system.

The family system is organized by certain roles, responsible behaviors, and family hierarchy. Family traditions, stories or myths, expectations, and style are all part of the system and give members a sense of purpose and equilibrium. To maintain a steady state of functioning or homeostasis, family members will consciously or unconsciously strive to return to what is most familiar, to rebalance the family to its original, familiar state. From this perspective it can be seen that within a family change is difficult to achieve and maintain. This can be a comforting insight to families, including church families, when we are in the process of change, to remember that by nature structural changes take time.

The cornerstone of Bowen's theory is differentiation of self. To be differentiated as a person is to be able to balance thoughts and feelings while acting, instead of reacting impulsively to the environment. When we are differentiated we act as separate people, and at the same time respond in caring ways that sustain relationships. Healthy relationships are seen as interdependent instead of codependent or dependent.

Differentiation in the family system allows for individuality and freedom of choice while promoting and sustaining caring ways of being with the other. Intimacy is known through the ability to be with the other in a way that respects individual beliefs and values.

Another important concept of family systems theory is boundary.[38] Clear boundaries in a family occur when expectations, roles, and personal space are respected. Differentiated individuals know that they are in control of and responsible for themselves. In the case of parents and children, clear roles indicate parental responsibility for children. Leon and Leah will find it important to have more flexible boundaries to help Lisa as a young adult grow in self-confidence as Lisa handles more and more responsibilities on her own.

In our families we learn through our parental figures the meaning of marriage, gender roles, what it is to be a parent, our attitudes and beliefs about sexuality, and also what God is like. Gender patterns in family relationships are further explored in the book *The Invisible Web* by Marianne Walters, Betty Carter, Peggy Papp, and Olga Silverstein, who have done extensive work with the Women's Project in Family Therapy.[39] In our families, destructive and constructive patterns are established. Was there a clear message that children were important to the family and should be both seen and heard? Each family system supports unique values and understandings of the world.

How does an understanding of family systems apply to ministry? Can the congregation be thought of as a family system that functions interdependently? Edwin Friedman and Peter Steinke helpfully use Murray Bowen's family systems theory to explore the family systems of churches and synagogues. Were Pastor Leon to read more about family systems theory as it may apply to the Leesville congregation, he might learn some additional ways of decreasing reactivity within the congregation and increasing the ability of his members to think clearly and objectively.

An Interpersonal Covenant

Leon may find that reading about systems theory and other resources will help his understanding of his congregation, but an equally important commitment will be his willingness to think through the way in which his personal family history might be impacting his ministry at this time. For every minister, there may be value in considering the following questions and then making an interpersonal covenant that represents a next growth step in self-awareness and understanding:

Interpersonal Covenant

In my personal and family history, *what did I learn about men and women? What did I learn about marriage and family, including the care of children? What did I learn about love and loving relationships (parents, siblings, classmates, neighborhood friends)? What kinds of interpersonal limits were identified? Were interpersonal limits respected in my home? How was discipline handled? How was conflict experienced and managed?*

Now, as an adult, *what do I recognize in my present life that is a reflection of my experiences growing up in my family? How have my years in ministry reinforced my early learnings?*

Do I have someone (a professional or a friend or a colleague) with whom I can discuss my interpersonal history? What difference does it make that I do or that I don't? If I don't have someone to talk with, would it be helpful to establish such a relationship as part of a covenant to make with myself?

My covenant *in the social dimension of my personhood, particularly in my marriage/family and/or my most significant interpersonal relationships, which could lead to my growth as a relational person in Christ:*

5

COVENANT & SPIRITUALITY

BEARERS OF THE LIGHT

Jesus said "I am the light of the world," a Light that the darkest of nights cannot extinguish. Matthew reminds us that we who follow Jesus carry this light of Christ with us. Through our witness, we "are the light of the world" (John 8:12, Matthew 5:14). As a Christian minister, Leon is called to be a bearer of the light of Christ so that those he serves will not stumble in the darkness.

There are three times when ministers have an especially hard time being a bearer of the light. One is when the darkness deepens, one is when the light seems to be fading, and a third is when it looks like everything is bright and no light seems to be needed. Let's consider each of these three challenges to ministry.

When No Light Seems Needed

Let's begin with the challenge Leon is *not* facing: when everything is bright and no light seems needed. There are times in ministry when the reverse of Leon's experience is true: there are no financial problems, attendance is up and growing, relationships are going well within the parish and at home, there are many opportunities and options, and the minister is feeling competent and in control.

Why it is a challenge to ministry rather than simply an occasion for rejoicing is that it is much easier to forget our dependence on God when things are going so well. This is not a new challenge for God's people. The Book of Deuteronomy cautions: "And it will be, when the LORD your God shall have brought you into the land . . . then beware lest you forget the Lord . . ."(Deut. 6:10-12).

The role of the minister when everything is fine is to help those who are enjoying the benefits of good times to remember the Source of all good things. If the minister forgets from whom all blessings flow, then the blessings of life can feel like the triumph of ingenuity and the human spirit rather than the gift and indwelling of the Holy Spirit.

Leon is not feeling very ingenious right now. His is rather the challenge to ministry that occurs when darkness deepens and the light fades.

When the Darkness Deepens

A minister is also challenged when the darkness deepens and it seems as if whatever light exists is not enough to overcome the depth of that darkness. In congregational terms, this is what seems to happen when the parish is overwhelmed with one difficult situation coming on top of another. It sometimes feels, not only to members of a congregation but also to ministers, as if heaven (the usual direction to look for help) has opened up and dumped on them personally.

That is how Leon is feeling right now. Leon left a budding business career because he did not like the competitive atmosphere in which there were winners and losers. Right now, he is feeling like a loser. While his first two congregations went pretty well, Leon simply does not know how to deal with the pressures affecting the Leesville church. His earlier training in business helps him see the economic handwriting on the wall. The worst is yet to come. More and more of his members will be losing their jobs and their financial security. As that happens, offerings will decrease even further.

If the economic downturn did not threaten his own security, perhaps Leon would feel more able to rise to the challenge and increase his pastoral care and support of those whose lives were being affected by these community changes. However, his own salary has been capped and he suspects that at the next congregational meeting a salary cut will be recommended. With Leah's income already only half of what it was, Leon is turning inward with survival anxiety. Rather than being more available for his parishioners, which is what is needed from a pastoral perspective, Leon is less available. His mind is elsewhere. There seems to be little light shining in this darkness, and the darkness is deepening.

One possible source of support during times of darkness is from immediate family and friends. Unfortunately, Leon is in a situation where the problems he faces also directly affect his family. If Leah's work were secure, the overall impact on the family would be lessened. As it is, she can do nothing to alleviate Leon's economic concerns since her own job is in jeopardy. In addition, Leah is not very happy with Leon right now and Leon is feeling quite unconnected at home. Their marriage is stressed. Leah feels she and the children are being neglected. Their son's school problems, which may be a reflection of the tension at home, only add to the pressure Leon is feeling.

Feeling threatened vocationally and lacking a refuge at home leaves Leon feeling overwhelmed. Alcohol does nothing to lighten the darkness, although Leon associates his drinking with relief from stress. If he has a predisposition to chemical addiction, the alcohol could deepen the darkness even more. Feeling inadequate as a pastor, husband, and father, Leon is all the more vulnerable to boundary crossing with a parishioner who sees him positively and affirms him as a pastor and as a man.

When the Light Fades

A third challenge to ministry is when the light fades. This may happen even if the environment is not one of deepening darkness. For example, Leesville could be a thriving community with a healthy and supportive congregation, and still the light within Leon could begin to fade. Alcoholism and other drug dependency, immobilizing anxiety attacks, and biochemical depression occur not only in parishioners but also in pastors even when the world around them is vibrant with life and possibility. When a person is struggling within, the promises of faith may seem far from being fulfilled. While theologians suggest that faith sees best in the dark, when the light within fades, faith may not see at all. When Jacob was wrestling with God at the River Jabbock, he wrestled throughout the night. A blessing came in the morning, but during the night there was only the battle.

Sometimes a minister is too tired to battle any longer. That may be a sign of fading light, which can lead to depression or can be the result of depression. Some may think that Leon could be doing a lot more about his situation than he is doing. There are, however, a number of things that can get in the way of a minister feeling able to get on top of a problem. One possibility is that Leon is not just frustrated and stressed or burning out, but that Leon is actually depressed at the present time.

Consider some typical symptoms of depression as they could appear in any person, but also in a pastor like Leon. There are often physical symptoms of tiredness or exhaustion, a feeling of heaviness in the body, a feeling of being slowed down. This is frequently accompanied by a change in appetite. Some people gain weight when depressed, many lose weight. A change in sleeping habits also may be a sign of depression. Some who are depressed are tired and want to sleep all the time. Many have difficulty falling asleep or they awaken during the night or awaken much earlier than usual and are not able to get back to sleep. The change in sleep can be in one direction or another, or one problem can follow the other, but some change in sleep patterns is common.

During depression, the use of alcohol or other forms of self-medication may also increase. To be depressed is to be in psychic pain, and when people, including pastors, are in pain they usually try to reduce their discomfort. Alcohol is one of the primary substances used in our society to get some relief.

Depression also changes the way we think of ourselves, sometimes drastically. A negative self-image is not uncommon in ministers who are depressed, or who have feelings of inadequacy and low self-esteem. One is likely to feel self-critical and unable to accomplish as much as usual at home or at work. The lowered opinion of oneself that accompanies feelings of failure can be compounded by feeling unmotivated to do the kinds of things that would have to be done for things to be any different, including taking initiative. Feelings of isolation from those at home and from pastoral colleagues at work are also common among ministers who are depressed.

Mentally as well as physically, a minister may notice a slowing down. It may be harder to concentrate and easier to forget things, even important things. Sermon writing, staying on task, thinking of new ideas or alternatives—all are likely to be much harder. When these things happen, a minister may be prone both to greater defensiveness and to feeling even more incompetent and unequal to the task. This can lead to feelings of worthlessness as a person as well as a pastor.

Spiritually, what happens when the keeper of the vision is lacking in vision, not only personally but also for the congregation and for the family at home? At deeper levels, helplessness can give way to hopelessness and despair. Is life itself worthwhile? A minister's personal and vocational identity is based on life's deeper meaning. If the minister and messenger of meaning loses a sense of the meaningfulness of life, there is little perceived light in the midst of darkness.

It is a significant challenge to ministry when the herald of hope loses hope. At those times, it is crucial for the minister to reach out to others outside the congregation to receive ministry. A pastoral colleague or perhaps a professional like a family physician or a counselor could be very helpful to Leon right now. Unfortunately, his greater sense of isolation makes it even more difficult for Leon to reach out, even though God provides so many resources for us in times of trouble—both within and outside the church. As identified in prior chapters, Leon seems to have many of the symptoms of depression and he has lost a sense of the unity of life that flows from God's covenant with all creation.

GOD'S COVENANT WITH CREATION

God's covenant is made with Abraham and Sarah, with Moses, and with David. In addition to these three, there is also a fourth and very important understanding of covenant reflected in Old Testament theology; God covenants with *all of creation!* Such an idea is hinted at when Hosea thinks of God making a covenant "with wild animals, the birds of the air, and the creeping things of the ground." Isaiah similarly thinks of a covenant with universal significance, whose violation leaves the entire cosmos lying polluted (Isa. 24:4-6).

The idea of God's universal covenant with all of creation becomes most pronounced in the theological reflection of Israel's priestly tradition. Unlike the earlier Deuteronomic tradition, whose concept of covenant focused narrowly upon Moses and Mt. Sinai, this tradition reintroduced the character of Abraham, but gave a radical new significance to the notion of an Abrahamic covenant. In the earlier epic tradition, the covenant with Abraham was focused exclusively upon God's promise of the Land of Canaan to Abraham and Sarah and their descendants (Gen. 12:17-21). When the later Priestly tradition once again took up this theme, however, it gave it a universal and cosmic twist. It promised not a specific land but rather a multitude of nations" (Gen. 17:1-8).

What is more important is that this Priestly notion of God's covenant with Abraham and Sarah is carried back further into history, so that it is essentially a renewal of the covenant that God had already made with Noah following the catastrophic flood (Gen. 9:1-17). Notice how the language of being fruitful and multiplying links these two covenants together. Finally, this same language is characteristic of the story of creation in Genesis 1, where God blesses animals and humans with the charge "to be fruitful and multiply" (Gen. 1:22, 28). For this Priestly tradition the covenant with Abraham and Sarah is nothing less than the renewal of the covenant with Noah and ultimately the renewal of God's very act of the creation of the world itself. The creation of the world in Genesis 1, the re-creation of the world with Noah in Genesis 9, and the new creation of the world community under God's care with Abraham in Genesis 17 are all closely tied together in the Priestly understanding of covenant.

Why did the Priestly view operate with this perspective? If the epic tradition about Abraham and Sarah and the land of Canaan was forged during the period of the Solomonic enlightenment and the Deuteronomic tradition about Moses and the covenant at Sinai was shaped by Israel's loss of national status, the Priestly tradition connecting Abraham to Noah and creation was forged in the context of the total collapse of temple, monarchy, and national existence. A sea of chaos had swept over Judah with its defeat and exile by the armies of Babylon, returning God's promise to the primal state of a formless void (Gen. 1:2). But just as God once drew order and design out of the chaotic void, so those standing in the void of Babylonian exile believed that the conditions were right for God to repeat this stupendous miracle of creation. They were now fundamentally landless. What better figures could symbolize their condition than that of Abraham and Sarah, whom the ancient epic tradition had already celebrated as the bearer of the promise of land? But Israel had not simply lost land in its fight with Babylon. It had lost its entire reality, its entire world view, its entire cosmos. This is why the figures of Abraham and Sarah are once again taken up, but now are seen within the context of a flow that leads back through Noah's restoration following the flood all the way to the very act of God's primal creation itself. The concept of covenant as adopted in the Priestly tradition indeed has cosmic and universal dimensions. The covenant made with Abraham and Sarah is nothing less than the rehearsal of the covenant that God had made with all creation when, in the beginning, God created the heavens and the earth.

GRACEFUL WAYS TO
KEEP COVENANT WITH GOD
True Spirituality

The covenants with Abraham and Sarah, Moses, David, and all creation reveal a God who reaches out in so many ways and surrounds us with love. How do we respond to the God who makes a covenant with creation except by being stewards of creation? As part of creation, but even more as those to whom God's world has been entrusted, we take care of God's creative handiwork. From this perspective, taking care of ourselves is one of the ways we take care of God's creation. Faithful self-care is an expression of spirituality.

The covenants with Abraham and Sarah, Moses and David, connect much more specifically with our Judeo-Christian heritage. The family of faith is traced prior to Jesus' time to Abraham and Sarah, Isaac and Rebekah, Jacob and Rachel. The family is present in the narratives of Jesus' birth and the first chapter of Matthew linking Jesus through David all the way back to Abraham and Sarah. Luke goes further, tracing the lineage of Jesus back to Adam.

True spirituality comes from God and embraces all with whom God is or would be in covenant. Spirituality is sometimes misunderstood when three terms are confused and used interchangeably: the spiritual, spirituality, and spiritual disciplines or expression. These are not synonymous terms, as each of them conveys something very specific and special.

A definition of the word "spiritual" that incorporates the Judeo-Christian sense of family as well as the family of creation can be inferred from Ephesians 3:14-19:

> For this reason I bow my knees before (God), from whom every family in heaven and on earth is named, that according to the riches of (God's glory God) may grant you to be strengthened with might through (the) Spirit in the inner (person), and that Christ may dwell in your hearts through

faith; that you, being rooted and grounded in love, may have power to comprehend with all the saints what is the breadth and length and height and depth, and to know the love of Christ which surpasses knowledge, that you may be filled with all the fullness of God.

In *God's Gifted People*, the spiritual is defined as

The height, length, breadth, and depth of the love of God that underlies, embraces, and transforms our personal and communal life together. Christians believe that God's love has been most clearly and gracefully revealed in Christ Jesus. Note that the symbol of the cross is created vertically (height and depth) and horizontally (length and breadth). The spiritual nature of life is not ours to design or develop. It is a gift of God.[40]

When all of life is comprehended as the gift of the Spirit, then it is not possible for us to think of spirituality as a *part* of life, or something that we do. It is more biblical to think of spirituality as the way we see life. We might say that spirituality is "seeing with the eyes of faith."[41] At the heart of what we experience in our physical life, at the heart of our thinking and feeling and relating, we see "with the eyes of faith" the presence and the power of God. No good thing is possible apart from the Spirit and so in every good thing we see God's presence if we choose to look through the eyes of faith.

Our spirituality also has a behavioral component. Once we see what God has done and is doing, we want to express our thanks. There are many ways to do this. Faithful self-care is one way. Being a good steward of other facets of God's created world is another. Within the holy catholic church, the communion of saints, the traditional ways to express our spirituality are through spiritual disciplines such as worship, the study of Scripture, and prayer. In most of Christendom the proclamation of the Word and the administration of the Sacraments of Baptism and the Lord's Supper are recognized as ways through which spirituality is nurtured. However, because God bestows different gifts on different persons, it is to be expected that some forms of spiritual expressions will come more naturally to some than to others. The rituals of worship may be very different, but spirituality is not to be confused with how we express our spirituality. At the heart of these various forms of worship is a common Christian perception that God is at the center of life and Christ the embodiment of grace.

Spirituality is not something we can do; true spirituality, then, can come only as a gift of God since we can see only as God gives us grace to see. Martin Luther saw even our faith as a grace gift: "I believe by my own reason or strength I cannot believe in Jesus Christ, my Lord, or come to him. But the Holy Spirit has called me through the Gospel. . . ."[42]

Once we see, however, we must choose what we shall do about what we see. All forms of spiritual expression, therefore, are not ways to God, but ways to give thanks to God because through Christ God has given the Way to us.

Seeing with Eyes of Faith

Leon is having a hard time seeing God's presence and power in his life and ministry at Leesville. Anyone who has walked through a valley of the shadow knows that it can be very difficult, at times, to see through the eyes of faith.

What are some of the results of seeing with the eyes of faith? Studies of seminarians and of ministers often reveal many signs of stress.[43] The symptoms are very similar to what Pastor Leon is now experiencing: stress, anxiety, fatigue, and other psychophysiological symptoms of distress.

These same studies have shown that it makes a world of difference what a person sees during these stressful times. It has been recommended that stress-management training for clergy be accompanied by coping skills development, including the "building of support networks, reducing the stigma of seeking professional support, and reframing (improving their ability to view their circumstances in more positive terms)."[44]

From a spiritual perspective, this reframing needs to take a special, cruciform shape. Seeing new possibilities, looking beyond the wall to a larger vision, is possible when seen at the heart of life is the height and depth, length and breadth of the love of God in Christ Jesus. The kind of faith that really seems to make a difference is when change is perceived as a challenge rather than as a threat, when a person believes that God will provide alternative ways when the way seems blocked, and when Christ is perceived as a very real and caring presence in stressful times; it has been shown in statistical studies that anxiety is significantly lower in persons who positively (faithfully) reappraise what is going on in their lives.[45]

A Spiritual Covenant

Biblically considered, the spiritual is never simply a *part* of life. Rather, it is at the *heart* or *center* of life. To summarize: we look to the Spirit as the presence and power of God. The movement of Spirit is from God to us. Spiritual expression is a movement from us to God, such as when we pray to God or do other things to express our faith. Spirituality is more than a prayerful or worshipful expression. Rather than something we do, spirituality is actually a way of seeing. To see with the eyes of faith would be to see ourselves through Christ's eyes of compassionate love and to see others in the same way. To see with the eyes of faith is to perceive the presence and power of God at the heart of the ordinary physical, mental, emotional, and social dimensions of life. Because of the movement of the Spirit to us, those whose eyes are opened to see are able to see God at the center of life.

To see with the eyes of faith is to see that doubt is not the opposite of faith, but rather doubt is an element of faith. Doubt does not mean all is lost, but is a sign of our need to nourish faith so that our hope can be restored.

If Leon wanted to make a covenant of spiritual care it could be helpful to take a look at some of the things that could interfere with the keeping of such a covenant. Whether you are working through this book alone or with a covenant study group, please take a few minutes now to ask the following questions.

Spiritual Covenant

> While growing up, *what was my experience with church or religion? What was my picture of God as a child? What was taught about God in my family? What did I learn about law and gospel from my pastor and/or other significant religious leader(s)?*
>
> *Do I have time in my day for quiet reflection and focus on the spiritual in relationship to* myself *rather than only to those I serve? In what ways does being a religious leader* enhance *the expression of my spirituality? In what ways does being a religious leader make meaningful expression of spirituality* more difficult? *If there is potential for the physical, emotional, mental, and social*

dimensions of my personhood to put me in touch with my spiri-
tuality, in which of these areas of my personhood is my spiritual-
ity most naturally experienced and/or expressed?

Now, as an adult, *what do I recognize in my present life that*
is a reflection of my experiences growing up in my family? How
has my experience in ministry reinforced my early learnings?

Do I have someone (a professional or a friend or a colleague)
with whom I can discuss my spiritual history? What difference
does it make that I do or that I don't? If I don't have someone to
talk with, would it be helpful to establish such a relationship as
part of a covenant I make with myself?

My covenant *which could lead to my growth as a spiritual*
person in Christ:

PART TWO

COVENANT & MINISTRY

6

COVENANT & CONFLICT

CONGREGATIONS IN CONFLICT
Alligators, Antagonists, and Such

In Florida they are sometimes called alligators. In more parts of the church they are known as antagonists.[46] When ministers talk with each other about parishes and parishioners and mention having to cope with an antagonist, the other ministers in the group may smile a certain smile and nod their heads.

Congregational conflict is something that all of us know about, but most ministers hate to experience. Pastor Leon is no exception. He did not become a pastor so he could fight with people. Like most pastors, he does not enjoy conflict and avoids it whenever he can.

The reasons that alligators or antagonists are so dismaying to ministers is that the terms refer to a parishioner who precipitates conflict with the *intention* of doing so. Rather than looking for solutions, the alligator or antagonist is looking for a problem.

Sadly, some people seem to fit the description of an antagonist. For whatever reasons, whether it be past personal history or previous sour congregational experience or something else, there are a few people who stir up trouble with every intention to stir up trouble.

It is a mistake, however, to assume that all conflict in a congregation is the work of an antagonist. Conflict can in fact be very healthy and necessary, at times. It is not conflict itself that is a problem, but what we do when conflict arises that can cause a problem. To see all who challenge a position as an antagonist or to label all who question the preferences of the minister as an alligator would be most self-defeating, because sometimes a congregation can only grow and become healthier by working through conflicting opinions about how to be the church most effectively and faithfully. If ministers react to all conflict as if conflict were in and of itself bad, the opportunities for learning and growing that can come out of conflict will be lost.

What are some of the sources of conflict other than when an antagonist is at work or an alligator is biting? Two of the more common causes of conflict are related to a congregation's history and to a changing context.

Family Fights

Some congregations have a history of fighting within the congregational family. Two of the reasons for a history of conflict within a congregation are not knowing how to fight fairly, and having something in the congregation's history that just won't go away. When there is this kind of history, the present fighting is a symptom of something deeper from the past.

First, just as in our family when we were growing up, a congregational family can have a history of fighting without knowing how to fight fairly. To fight fairly we need to identify clearly what we are upset about, why it upsets us, what is needed to make things right, and what it will take to make things work better. Many of us learn in our family of origin not to complain about things, but to put up with what we do not like as long as we can. Consequently, we may build up quite a bundle of complaints before ever saying something. When we do, whatever was the final straw can lead us to react way out of proportion. What we are really reacting to is not just the final straw, but all that preceded the final straw.

Not surprisingly, the one who experiences our reaction may see it as an *overreaction*. The intensity of our reaction is increased when we add our feelings about all that preceded the final straw to our feelings at the moment we experience the final straw. Since an overreaction may come through also as an attack, it may lead the other person to mount a counterattack. The counterattack usually introduces more heat than light, so it is not uncommon that it will lead to a counterattack to the counterattack. Little may be resolved by this sequence of events, and both parties may walk away feeling very misunderstood and maligned. In such a situation, it is not an antagonist that is involved, but simply faulty learning about how to resolve conflicts in a timely and reasonable way.

The second reason for congregational fighting is more subtle and often unrecognized. If a congregation has had a significant disruption in its history and there are unresolved feelings about that disruption, those feelings do not just go away. Present day fighting may be related to those unresolved feelings, even though the parties to the conflict may not realize it at the time.

Some congregations have a history of difficulty with their pastors. In such congregations, pastors tend to come and go, with relatively short and troubled ministries. Although the new pastor looks like the answer to the congregation's problems, for one reason or another things turn sour.

When there is a pattern of such abbreviated or troubled ministries, it is not uncommon to find in the past history of the congregation a particularly traumatic experience that was emotionally charged at the time and never completely resolved. For example, a former minister may have been accused of misappropriation of funds or sexual misconduct or some other behavior incompatible with the pastoral office. Such charges often result in deep divisions within the congregation between supporters and detractors. Regardless of how the situation turns out, everyone seems to lose and the emotions run high. If the congregation simply tries to forget the event and focus on the future, the grieving process may never be completed. Trust is hard to regain and the next pastors will not be considered trustworthy just because they are pastors.

When the congregational history includes periods of alleged or actual broken trust, then the climate is right for all kinds of actions on the part of the minister to be questioned about motivation. Even though nothing is wrong, even the smallest things can lead to eruptions that are out proportion to what has just occurred. What is fueling the eruption is much more than what has just occurred. It is all that history and any unresolved feelings about that history.

Unfortunately, those involved in such conflicts may not realize that it is really the past that is pressing into the present conflict for emotional release. The sign that more is going on than what is here and now is the disproportion of the reaction to the present situation. Because those involved in the conflict may not consciously be thinking of the past event, they do not make that connection. They may only be aware of feeling very angry with the minister and with the way things are done in their congregation.

In all likelihood, until the past is re-opened and feelings ventilated about whatever occurred, the congregation will not fully heal from past hurts. One of the most important things a new pastor can do when entering a congregation is to learn the congregational history, its high points, and its low points. If there is a past low point that remains unresolved, there may well be another low point ahead.

The Times Are Changing

In addition to the agenda of antagonists and the role of personal or congregational history, a third precipitant of conflict is when the context of ministry is undergoing a major change. Changes in the context usually exert considerable pressure on a congregation.

Family systems theory has helped us to understand that congregational families experience dynamics similar to those within the family home. One of those dynamics is the resistance to change. When the homeostasis of the family is threatened, there is a powerful press to restore the familiar balance.

Resistance to change can show up when a congregation grows to the point where the pastor has trouble keeping the close, personal relationship with each member that was possible when the congregation was smaller. Arlin Rothauge describes the impact of congregational size in "Sizing Up a Congregation for New Member Ministry."[47] The patriarchal church, according to Arlin Rothauge, has fifty or less active members. The pastoral size congregation has from fifty-150. The program church has between 150 and 350, then the congregation becomes a corporate church (350 or more active members). For many congregations, the most difficult transition is the movement from a pastoral to a program church. That is the time when the relationship with the pastor takes on a different feel that is often, of necessity, less personal. Lay leaders assume additional leadership responsibilities and assume some pastoral functions as well. Both the pastor and the congregation may resist this movement to the program church. Powerful forces emerge, sometimes consciously and sometimes unconsciously, that may keep a congregation from growing to where the relationship with the pastor has to change.

Similar dynamics of resistance may appear when the congregation remains the same size, but the surrounding community or context is changing. The influx of persons from a different culture, even when there is an exodus of old timers from the congregation, does not necessarily result in an open door to persons from the new culture. There may be a tendency to maintain the old, familiar worship practices and hymns, even though those from a different culture would be more attracted to a service that incorporated elements of their culture's ways of worshipping and singing. At times this press to maintain the status quo can result in a church eventually having to disband. At other times, there may be considerable internal conflict as members struggle between the desire not to change and the desire to survive.

Change and conflict are inevitable and often traumatic. In times of conflict and change, a congregation needs prophetic leadership. Perhaps there is something that we can learn by looking more carefully at what prophetic leadership of the covenant community involves.

THE MINISTER/PASTOR AS PROPHET

What does it mean for the leaders of God's people to be in covenant with those they work with? Let's consider one of the three traditional models of leadership in the Old Testament: the prophet.

While there are many ideas about what it means to have a prophetic ministry, in the Old Testament the prophet functioned as a visionary, a healer, and as an intercessor on behalf of the religious community.

The Prophet as Visionary

The fundamental function the prophet had in Israelite society was to be a transmitter or conduit of information from the divine or trans-human realm that could not be gained by normal means. Two of the earliest labels for prophets in Israel were "seer" and "visionary."[48] For example, Samuel was able to "see" where Saul's lost donkeys were (1 Sam. 9:3-21) and Micaiah "saw" the outcome of a pending battle (1 Kgs. 22:17). Prophets were often asked to open a window into the divine world.

The Prophet as Healer

In Israel the prophet was also the one to whom people often went for healing. Recall the visit paid by the leprous Naaman to the prophet Elisha (2 Kings 5:1-14), or the healing of King Hezekiah by the fig poultice concocted by the prophet Isaiah (2 Kings 20:7). Such healing was also attributed to

Elijah and Elisha in resuscitating a boy from the dead (1 Kings 17:17-24; 2 Kings 4:18-37), and even to the bones of the dead Elisha, which were sufficiently powerful to bring another dead man back to life (2 Kings 13:20-21). The prophet as powerful healer, as one who was regarded to have a mysteriously charged force capable of focusing God's healing power, forms the background for the question posed by the religious leaders to the man born blind. Upon his having been healed by Jesus, the formerly blind man was asked, "Who do you say that he is?" The man responds as though it ought to be self evident, "Why, he is a prophet!" (John 9:17).

The Prophet as Intercessor

Because of the extraordinary power thought to be exerted by the prophet's ability to convey information from the realm of the divine and to control the forces of weal and woe, the prophet was also considered to be an intercessor on behalf of the community. Kings would often come to the prophet asking not only for information concerning the future but also to see if the prophet would be willing to plead to God on behalf of the people. King Hezekiah made several such calls on the prophet Isaiah (2 Kings 19:1-7; 14-34) as did King Zedekiah on the prophet Jeremiah (Jer. 37:3-10; 38:14-23). The commander Johanan ben Kareah specifically requested Jeremiah to "pray to the Lord" on behalf of the people (Jer. 42:2). Certainly individuals could and did go directly to God in petitionary prayer. However, it was universally acknowledged that the prophet had a particular power. Having a prophet as intercessor on your behalf was thought to improve considerably the odds of a favorable divine hearing.

In a prophetic ministry, the pastor is the community's chief healer and intercessor. Rather than simply pointing out the community's wound in accusatory tones, the prophet is willing to make the fig poultice or take in hand the leprous limb or rub the mud and spittle in the blind eye in order to effect healing. Rather than simply highlighting the community's brokenness and taking sides with God against them, the prophet must first be willing to be an all-out advocate on behalf of the people as their chief intercessor with God. It is only as a result of such intercession *on behalf of the people* that the minister has a right to issue a word of opposition in the name of God. It is only as a result of the minister sharing humanity's wounds and fears and frustrations that the minister gains the privilege of calling for healing and restoration.

The prophet, as the conduit of the divine word, surely was charged with the task of speaking that word within the community's hearing. It is very tempting, however, to romanticize our view of the rugged individualist who fractures the peace of the community from the outside. Such a romanticized notion of the function of the prophet has been shaped by three principle factors: the Reformation's legacy of focusing on the pure word over against human tradition and cultic ritual; the Enlightenment's elevation of individual rationality; and Romanticism's fascination with the noble savage or the Nietzschean superman. In fact, the role of the prophet is not that of fracturing the convictions of the community as a hammer from the outside. Rather the appropriate function of the prophet is that of stretching the vision of the community from the inside, of recalling the community to its central vision, its formative story, its own mythic consciousness, and of extrapolating the meaning of that vision for the life of the community, even if it sometimes appears that the community is being stretched to the breaking-point.

PROPHETIC COVENANT-KEEPING

Ministry as a prophetic covenant-keeping involves our allowing God to work through us in ways that resonate with the three prophetic roles of seer, healer, and intercessor.

Seeing Is Perceiving

The minister as seer, or as one who opens a window into the divine world, calls upon us to see what is going on around us in a special way. Psychologists tell us that perception plays a powerful role in human behavior. You may have seen in a psychology textbook the figure of an hourglass (or vase) which, when looked at differently, can also be perceived as two persons face to face. The basic learning is that, if something can be perceived in at least two ways, it really makes a difference which way we see it. From a cognitive-behavioral standpoint, we react to what we see. If we perceive something as a threat, we react with anxiety or fear. If we perceive the same thing as less a threat than an opportunity, we react with excitement and enthusiasm.

Research in the 1980s introduced the concept of faith-hardiness.[49] A hardy faith is one where, trusting in the grace of God in Christ Jesus, change is perceived as a challenge, every situation is seen as holding options and alternatives (if only an alternative way to react to a given, such as terminal illness), and Christ is seen as a very real presence even in the darkest and most stressful situations. Faith-hardiness is not a Pollyanna faith, nor is its power the power of positive thought. It does not deny the cross, but enters into the darkness with courage born of faith that the darkest darkness cannot overcome the Light of Christ. In research studies, the faith-hardy have significantly lower anxiety levels and are less subjectively stressed even when circumstances are very difficult.

A prophetic ministry sees the hand of God leading God's people, even though the paths are not always clear and the perils not completely identified and the end is still in question as to how things will turn out. The courage to face all this uncertainty comes not from faith in our own ability to manage the unmanageable or cope with the uncopable. Rather, the courage comes from faith in God's being present to guide and support us with love through the process of our moving toward an indefinite future.

Pastor Leon is much more aware of the *threat* to the congregation and to him personally than he is conscious of the *challenge* and *opportunity* that the present problem provides. All around him, Pastor Leon sees real or anticipated loss, with tomorrow likely to bring worse news. He is in a survival mode, worried that if he does not personally assure his economic future then all may soon be lost.

When ministers no longer are prophetically seeing through the threats that surround us to the opportunities that God's promises provide, then God's people are also more likely to slip into the survival mode as well. The more afraid people are, the less likely they are to see options and alternatives because anxiety tends to narrow our vision rather than expand it.

To see as the prophet sees is an expression of a spirituality that perceives the presence and power of the Holy Spirit at the center of the ordinary as well as the extraordinary. Everyday problems of paying bills and other obligations and of having fewer volunteers than are needed to carry out the congregation's ministries pose a threat, to be sure, but such problems are also a challenge.

When a minister cannot see past the threat to the challenge, joining with other ministerial colleagues in a support group can be very helpful. Christina Maslach, one of the leading researchers in caregiver burnout, found that "burnout rates are lower for those professionals who actively express, analyze, and share their personal feelings with their colleagues."[50] She especially found to be helpful "peer group meetings . . . where workers can talk over their fears, doubts, and get needed support and positive feedback."

One of the real values of colleague groups is that members can help one another see past the threats to the challenge. When there appears to be very limited options, and when God does not seem to be answering prayers for help, another colleague can listen and share a faithful reappraisal of the situation. The light and hope of Christ can then shine through. At some point, every member of the group is likely to have times when it is difficult to see problems through the eyes of faith. By being there for each other, colleagues can be a part of the fulfillment of Christ's promise to be with us always, and Christ's promise that he will not leave us comfortless.

Pastor Leon's relative isolation from his pastoral colleagues limits their ability to be there for him during this troubling time. Ideally, a minister finds a group of supportive colleagues *prior* to a crisis. Then, when a crisis occurs, there is an environment of trust already established strong enough for a minister to share feelings of inadequacy and of being overwhelmed without fear of being judged incompetent. The honest sharing of feelings and opening of oneself to help is a crucial first step in collegial support. Without such risk-taking, it is hard even for good hearted and supportive colleagues to respond in the most helpful ways.

While it might be even more helpful to have a *group* of colleagues to whom Pastor Leon could turn, he at least has an individual relationship with Pastor María upon which he might be able to draw. If between the two of them they were able to identify at least one or two other colleagues with whom they felt reasonably comfortable, they would have the makings of a support group. Until then, Pastor María might be able to help Pastor Leon see past the perils unknown to the guiding hand and supportive love of God in Christ Jesus.

The Hand that Bites

Since our perceptions play such a large part in how we manage a given situation, the way we see an interaction with another influences how we respond. This is especially true in the way ministers deal with criticism and conflict. Since criticism and conflict are inevitable in any organization, including a congregation, the way we see conflict and criticism is a key to handling it effectively. For instance, if Pastor Leon perceives criticism to be threatening, he is more likely to be on guard and ready to defend himself from attack. While taking such a stance might feel justified and self-protective, it limits our ability to think creatively and clearly in ways that lead to a resolution of the conflict. On the other hand, if Pastor Leon sees a situation of conflict and criticism as a challenge and an opportunity, he will be better equipped to manage whatever comes his way.

Criticism that feels like a personal attack can cause us to lose sight of the greater picture of the ministry that Jesus has called us to in the church. To put criticism in perspective, it may be helpful to refer back to systems theory. From a systems perspective we know that conflict is part of any family or organization. We can expect that a congregation will go through periods of conflict. We could say that conflict is the system's way of managing differences of perspective. A variety of perspectives and gifts can bring health to an organization or system if we can respect the differences. Often seminary does not equip ministers to manage criticism. Learning to handle conflict and criticism in the ministry in a healthy way is a key for surviving and thriving in the ministerial role.

In addition to handling conflict effectively, the minister also has the challenge of caring for those very persons who create conflict. The care and feeding of critics is a worthwhile skill for ministers to develop because it provides for faithful ministry and for faithful self-care.

To deal with criticism and conflict, Fred Smith, in "The Care and Feeding of Critics: How to Feed the Hand That Bites You,"[51] suggests keeping a number of things in mind. The first step in managing criticism is to expect that it will come—and it will probably come at inconvenient times. Ironically, when we have an inspirational program that we are enthusiastic about, criticism is sure to follow from others who have not captured the excitement. Criticism is also inevitable when there is a shift in power or recognition in the group or when a proposed change costs money or causes inconvenience. Just as an Olympian would expect and plan for pain, the leader is wise to expect criticism.

Pastors may find it helpful to identify *types* of critics in order to anticipate what the critic might say in a given situation. When we can see beyond our personal feelings and focus on identifying certain behaviors in the critic, we can deal with the situation more objectively and effectively. Smith mentions six classifications of critics: people who resent authority *per se* and "adhere to the bumper sticker slogan, Question All Authority;" people with natural leadership qualities who are not part of the majority, but if invited will use their gifts constructively; people who criticize to show their superior knowledge and who in fact could offer that expertise in a positive way if coached to do so; natural howlers, who are like hound dogs that prefer to lie on the cockleburr rather than move (the cockleburr being any new idea); people who use criticism to exorcise internal conflicts and are really in need of pastoral care for their hurts but can't ask for help directly; and genuine, honest, interested critics who feel responsible for the welfare of the organization. Genuine critics can be like buoys in the river that keep you in the channel and on course.

If criticism is anticipated and planned for, it can sometimes be defused and improve a project or idea. Smith says: "The key is to understand the base from which people work . . . we must know their deep beliefs, biases, experiences, theological positions, and especially their ego positions."[52] By understanding the person's internal logic, respect can be shown for the criticism while addressing the deeper need of the critic. The leader then clearly remains in the professional role of minister and avoids slipping into the personal role of taking the criticism to heart.[53]

If Pastor Leon can prophetically see past the danger to God's promise to be present, he will be all the more able to help turn this time of confusion and conflict into an opportunity for pastoral care and healing.

Stand by Me

A prophetic ministry incorporates not only the prophetic seer and the healer, but also the prophet's intercessory standing with, rather than over against, God's people. A covenantal minister loves first, then leads. The Alban Institute has been very helpful in letting persons new to ministry know that a congregation is concerned with whether or not a pastor cares.[54] It is hard to follow a pastoral leader whose love for you is questionable. Those who are led want to believe that their best interests are of concern to the one who leads them. Otherwise, why follow?

A friend is one who stands by us when the going gets rough. From the prophetic standpoint, it would be even stronger to say that a pastoral friend stands *with* us. The power of the pastoral office is to be used as a *power with*, rather than a power over those who are served. When power is used over others, exploitation may be a short step away. The calling of the pastor in a covenantal ministry is to be especially mindful of the weak and vulnerable, so that those who are most in need can be protected.

Pastor Leon needs to stand with his congregation and use the power of his office in their behalf. Because there are so many in the parish now hurting from the changes in their community and uncertain about the future, their pastor is all the more needed to be a person who understands their pain and who intercedes for them.

Pastor Leon's own pain during this time can result in his becoming increasingly self-absorbed with his own survival, or it can become an opportunity for him to enter into his pain as a way of better understanding what so many of those he serves are enduring. It is only by entering into the darkness that Pastor Leon can stand with his congregation. As one who *stands with*, the pastor can all the more raise a loving, intercessory voice to the God who promises to grace God's people with presence: "Even though I walk through the valley of the shadow of death, I fear no evil, for you are with me."

Once again, if he were a part of a colleague group of ministers, Leon could be supported and strengthened for his intercessory ministry in behalf of those who look to him for caring and leadership. As ministers allow other ministers to stand with them during the hard times, the way becomes even clearer as to how most effectively and faithfully to stand with their parishioners. Opening ourselves to receive makes it even more possible to comfort the comfortless with the comfort with which we ourselves have been comforted. (2 Cor. 1:3-4)

Standing with our parishioners will take on even more meaning as we now turn to the ministerial challenge of maintaining appropriate boundaries.

7

COVENANT & BOUNDARIES

SEX AND THE PARISH
Is Nothing Sacred?

We have talked about how clear boundaries in a family are created when expectations are clearly communicated, roles are well defined, and personal space is respected. Boundaries are limits that allow for a safe interpersonal connection. Limits are often perceived as inhibiting a relationship, but healthy boundaries actually facilitate relating. Boundaries provide for instead of take away from a relationship. Boundaries protect those whom we care about and care for by creating a safe place for everyone. Boundaries also define who we are—"where we leave off and the rest of the world begins, what is ours and not ours, what is intimate and what is separate."[55]

How can we respect one another's boundaries in our covenant relationships? How can we be clear in communicating our boundaries to others? How can an understanding of boundaries be helpful for Leon?

Pastor Leon is in danger of crossing a boundary with his parishoner, Flo. Her telephone invitation for him to come over to her place after work suggests that she is not considering his time with her as part of his work, but rather as an expression of their deepening relationship. His support and comfort during a difficult time in her life has led her to look upon him as someone she wants in an even more intimate way.

Pastor Leon is also in need of feeling valued and special. His need misdirected to Flo increases his risk of crossing the appropriate boundaries. He is beginning to think of Flo as his peer instead of his congregant. The turn of events in his community and the Leesville congregation have not only placed unexpected economic pressures on him, but have also affected his sense of self-esteem. He feels much less adequate as a person. He is barely able to keep up with the congregation's expectations at work and knows he is not being the spouse or parent he is expected to be at home. With Flo, Leon is feeling more competent as a pastor and more desirable as a person. With all these factors in mind, we see how Leon is in danger of crossing an ethical boundary with his parishoner.

Pastor Leon is having difficulty separating his own needs from his pastoral relationship to Flo. He is also in danger of reversing the roles of care giver and care receiver. When a pastor places his or her needs first and ahead of the parishoner there is a boundary violation, whether of a sexual or non-sexual nature. According to Marilyn R. Peterson, a boundary violation by a professional "dismantles the relationship, erases the limits and destroys the core intent of the connection between professional and client" (or parishoner).[56] In addition to the characteristic of reversed roles, a boundary violation is also secretive in nature. It also places the parishoner in a double bind where a move in or out of the relationship results in either loss of a pastor or a loss of emotional and/or physical safety.

Sex and Power

Even though Pastor Leon does not *feel* very powerful in his congregation at this time because of low self-esteem and conflict in the parish, power and authority are inherent in his role as pastor. A 1987 working document developed by the Northwest District of the American Lutheran Church reads:

> To be a pastor is to be entrusted with a sacred responsibility, to care for the church of God which was obtained with the blood of God's own Son. . . . Not only is the pastoral office a position of great trust and responsibility, it is also, by virtue of the trust persons place in the office and the person of pastor, a position of great authority and power over others.[57]

There is a power differential between Pastor Leon and Flo. No meaningful consent is possible when there is a power differential because of potential constraints on choice and potential coercion. The Center for the Prevention of Sexual and Domestic Violence resource entitled, "Not Just Consent . . . *Meaningful* Consent", states that meaningful consent requires equality of resources, lack of direct or indirect coercion, lack of constraints on choice, the ability to say "no" that requires confidence or maturity, and the freedom to say "no" (not punished, rejected, or shamed for saying "no").[58]

Flo is vulnerable in relation to Leon because he is her pastor. If Leon denies his power he will be more likely to disregard the impact of his behavior on Flo.[59] Flo seeks help in dealing with her grief at the anniversary of her father's birthday and in caring for her mother who she feels responsible to comfort and support. Flo looks to Leon for guidance, protection, and care while trusting that he will act in her best interest.

Because Leon has the power in relation to Flo, he has a responsibility to maintain boundaries even if those boundaries are pushed by her. Certainly she is needing someone to trust and draw stability from in this time of mourning her father and caring for her mother. The faithful way for Leon to care for Flo is to protect her vulnerability and not to take advantage of her need.

Peter Rutter, author of *Sex in the Forbidden Zone,* warns of the "inherently exploitative" nature of any sexual behavior within the forbidden zone. Because the pastor is the "keeper of the trust," it is the pastor's responsibility, no matter what the level of provocation or apparent consent by the congregant "to assure that sexual behavior does not take place."[60] Leon is responsible to use his power to protect Flo and all his other congregants and the integrity of the ministerial relationship.

In a discussion of power and models of ministry, The Center for the Prevention of Sexual and Domestic Violence delineates exercising "power over" from "power with." Power over is used to control others and to preserve clergy privilege. Power over originates in hierarchy and is accountable only to the hierarchy/structure. In a power with model of ministry, power is responsibly used to provide leadership and to protect the vulnerable. Power with originates in the community and is accountable to the community.[61]

The biblical witness suggests that "justice means upholding the powerless and holding accountable the powerful."[62] The primary concern of life together was life for the community that led consequently to life for the individual. No action was solely a private act, but everything affected everything else. True worship of God is not in solemn assemblies or burnt offerings but in kindness toward others. The prophet Amos declares the word of the Lord: "But let justice roll down like waters, and righteousness like an everflowing stream" (Amos 5:24).

Caring professionals subscribe in principle to the idea that what is good for the life of the community will lead to life for the individual and to the idea that what is done in the privacy of the helping relationship is not a private act, but something that affects everyone else. Consequently, helping professionals safeguard the community and the individual and the helping relationship by establishing a code of ethics.

Codes of ethics typically advocate the establishment of appropriate boundaries as those boundaries apply to the helping relationship and then go on to name what some of those appropriate boundaries should be. For example, the American Association for Marriage and Family Therapy (AAMFT) code of ethics states:

> Marriage and family therapists are aware of their influential position with respect to clients, and they avoid exploiting the trust and dependency of such persons. Therapists, therefore, should make every effort to avoid dual relationships with clients that could impair professional judgment or increase the risk of exploitation. . . . Examples of such dual relationships include, but are not limited to, business or close personal relationships with clients.[63]

In order to further safeguard the person seeking help, AAMFT professionals who help others are "to seek professional assistance for their (own) personal problems or conflicts that may impair work performance or clinical judgment."

Although there are some who resist the idea of a pastor being a professional, preferring to consider ministry as a vocation (calling) rather than a profession, there is something to be gained by recognizing that to the average layperson the minister is in a professional role. A pastor is one who has expertise in a particular area that requires advanced-level learning and mastery. A pastor is expected to act in the best interests of a parishoner rather than for personal gain or self-interest, and a pastor is expected to maintain an ethical standard that protects parishoners and to be self-monitoring. A pastor does not wait for outside regulation but actively and proactively seeks to protect those with whom they have a pastoral relationship.

These "professional" characteristics are ones that ministry as a vocation dare not be without. One might even believe that those in ministry must even go *beyond* what other helping professionals accept as minimum expectations because those called to the vocation of ministry do not do simply what professional rules require, but what is as loving as possible in response to the grace of God in Christ Jesus.

Dual Relationships

While Pastor Leon's relationship with Flo may be the most obvious boundary issue, it is certainly not the only one. Other boundary issues for Leon include the boundary between work and home, a changing boundary with his maturing daughter, and boundaries with alcohol use. Another important boundary issue is Leon's possible dual relationship between him and one of his congregants as a potential business partner.

A pastor is in a dual relationship when the pastor attempts to fulfill two roles with a parishoner. When Leon attempts to be Flo's pastor and her "nightcap and dessert partner" he is in a dual relationship.[64] He is also in a dual relationship if he attempts to be a business partner with one of his parishioners.

Dual relationships for health care professionals are strongly discouraged by most professional organizations. The American Association of Pastoral Counselors Code of Ethics recognizes the trust placed in and unique power of the therapeutic relationship.

> While acknowledging the complexity of some pastoral relationships, we avoid exploiting the trust and dependency of clients. We avoid those dual relationships with clients (e.g., business or close personal relationships) that could impair our professional judgment, compromise the integrity of the treatment, and/or use the relationship for our own gain. All forms of sexual behavior with clients are unethical, even when a

client invites or consents to such behavior or involvement. . . . We recognize that the therapist/client relationship involves a power imbalance, the residual effects of which are operative following the termination of the therapy relationship . . . therefore all sexual behavior or harassment . . . with former clients is unethical.

—AAPC Code of Ethics, 1994

In the American Association for Counseling and Development *Ethical Standards Casebook*, Karen Strohm Kitchener and Susan Stefanowski Harding write concerning dual role relationships: "Professionals . . . must be sensitive to emotional over-involvement that limits their ability to be appropriately objective or leads to the misuse of power."[65] The integrity of Pastor Leon's pastoral relationship with Flo is at risk when the boundary between pastor and parishoner is blurred.

The diligent and thorough attention to boundary issues in ministry is ultimately to safeguard our covenant relationships and edify the community in which we live, work, and play. In Old Testament writings, this attention to boundary issues is clearly reflected in the responsibilities of the priest.

THE MINISTER/PASTOR AS PRIEST

Both prophet and priest were called to remind God's people of their covenantal relationship with the creator and their responsibility to the community. Each had an area of competency in directing God's people back to the covenant. Both Jeremiah 18:18 and Ezekiel 7:26 indicate that the prophet was associated with the word or vision of God while the priest was connected with God's instruction or Torah. The prophet was called to be a Visionary, a Healer, and an Intercessor on behalf of the people of God. We could say that the prophet had these particular areas of competency. The vocation of the priest had other areas of competency, namely, to serve as omen reader, storyteller, and line judge.[66]

The Priest as Omen Reader

Urim and Thummim were the names of the sacral lots that were manipulated in some way by the priest in order to determine the answer to a particular question. It was characteristic throughout the ancient Near East that, through such means, priests gained information that was otherwise unobtainable. In many societies surrounding Israel omens were read by inspecting the livers of sacrificial animals, by casting arrows on the ground and reading their pattern, or by observing the nature of sacrificial smoke as it rose from the altar. The preferred method in Israel, it seems, was to gain such omens by reading the Urim and Thummim as they were cast, just as the lot was normally cast (Josh. 18:6).

The Priest as Storyteller

It may be in fact such casting that leads to the second area of competency, that of instruction. The verb for the casting of the Urim and Thummim, *yarah*, is directly related to the word for instruction, *torah*. Scholars debate whether the term *yarah* in this case means primarily to cast or throw, or rather to point out, as when one throws ones index finger forward at an object. In any case, there is undoubtedly a close connection between the priestly action of casting the sacred lots and pointing out the proper direction. Israel's torah, instruction, was the primary responsibility of the priest.[67]

As the teacher of the torah, the priest was Israel's chief storyteller. The task of the priest was to keep the story straight, to continue to hold before the people the essence of their God-given identity, and to remind them of that which was, as Walter Brueggemann says, "non negotiable" in their relationship with God and in their own constitutive identity.[68] The priest had primary catechetical responsibilities in regard to pilgrims seeking admission into worship. The priest was also involved in the resolving of legal disputes and in instructing the public concerning Israel's moral and ethical commitments, its ethos in life before God.

The Priest as Line Judge

The third major area of the priest's competency was to offer sacrificial animals to God and, as a corollary, to use the blood in rituals around the altar and sanctuary. What lay behind this function was the notion of marking off appropriate boundaries within the community, particularly the boundary between the realms of the holy and the common, the clean and the unclean.

When we think of what it means to be holy we often think of someone who is extremely religious or pious. But to be holy in Israel meant to be contaminated with the deadly power of God that naturally was exuded by God's presence. Encounter with the divine was thought to be lethal because of this holiness. God's presence among the people would be like a devouring fire if adequate precautions were not taken. Items that were contaminated by such holiness had to be scoured and decontaminated. God's presence in the midst of the people—symbolized by God's presence in the holy of holies in the temple—was like a nuclear reactor that, while generating life and energy for the people, was at the same time always a threatening presence.

Given this view, the priest was responsible for maintaining the integrity of both the sacral sphere associated with the divine presence and the common sphere where normal daily life was conducted. Disaster could result if either the holiness leaked out of the sacral sphere or if uncleanliness from the common sphere leaked into the temple precincts. Contamination was a two-way street, and its effects were thought to be potentially disastrous for the entire community. This is why the priest is commonly associated with making distinctions between the holy and the profane, and between the clean and the unclean. The priest had the primary responsibility for maintaining the boundaries of the community, both the boundary between the temple and the community (that is, the generative power of life that could contaminate it from within) and the boundary between the community and the world outside (that is, the deadly power of uncleanness that could contaminate it from without).

In summary, the priest was the chief omen reader, the community's storyteller, and the primary line judge. Above all, the priest was the one who mediated the divine presence with the torah.[69] If the prophet focused upon visionary and intuitive experience, the priest focused on tangible evidence before him, evidence that could be touched and manipulated, prodded and poked. The priest's world was not the world of intuition and imagination. The priest's world was the world of sifting through the hardcore material evidence. Thus, Jeremiah could refer to the priest as the one who handles the law (Jer. 2:8).[70]

The evocative vision of the prophet, as powerful as it might be, was fundamentally useless until filtered through the thoughtful framework of priestly analysis. The fiery passion of the prophetic word and the persistent reason of priestly torah complemented and corrected one another. But it was the priest who, as the one charged with the integrity of the community's boundaries, was ultimately responsible for making the volatile prophetic word usable.

As the community's priest the minister is charged with the integrity of the community's holiness, with making proper distinctions between that which is foundational for its identity and that which will infect it and will diminish the proclamation of the gospel. As such, the minister has the task of filtering potential words of God through the screen of received canons so as to make the diffused and potent word both concentrated and usable. The minister as priest is charged with keeping the story straight, with maintaining the integrity of the community's boundaries, and with providing the thoughtful voice of analysis that will give substance to the passion of the prophetic vision.

PRIESTLY COVENANT-KEEPING

Reading the Signs

When Leon was called to be pastor at Leesville Community Church, he accepted the opportunity and responsibility of providing a covenantal ministry. It was challenging, but Pastor Leon felt his ministry was going pretty well until the economic base of Leesville began to deteriorate. When Leon's salary was capped, he found it difficult to separate himself from the anxiety of his parishioners as they experienced unstable employment. How can Leon be the omen reader in his present situation? What kind of support will help Leon step back and objectively read the situation?

For Leon, and other ministers, help from his judicatory would facilitate meeting his personal needs so that he will be free to respond to his parishioners. For instance, a workshop on stress management or a seminar on how to set boundaries in ministry could provide helpful tools for self-care. His judicatory could assist him in further study through a bibliography outlining resources on sustaining a healthy marriage, parenting the adolescent, or meeting the challenges of mid-life. Providing a list of health care professionals in the Leesville area would also be a way for the judicatory to encourage self-care. With assistance, Leon could keep his priestly vocation alive and strong. Seeking out leadership support and consultation is self-care for the sake of ministry.

Telling the Story Straight

A priestly ministry tells God's story and proclaims the gospel, while holding before the people of God the essence of their God-given identity. For the Israelite, God's commitment and love were as fixed as the stars, as solid as the foundations of the earth, as eternal as the seas. When the Israelite looked into the heavens, the sun and stars and moon were reminders of God's creation of divine order out of chaos (Jer. 31:35-37).[71]

It was in this framework of God's commitment and love that Israel understood itself under the law, that indeed there existed a divine ordering and a holy intention of righteousness or right relationship with God.

In reality, God's covenant with us is simply a working out of this divine urge toward moral order characterized by the justice and righteousness of God that permeates the cosmos. Creation is the precondition for the covenant, not our obedience. Our relationship with God is not predicated upon our initiative and our ability to "keep the laws and obligations" of the covenant. Our relationship with God rests upon God's love renewed at every crisis point in human history. How could Leon nurture and strengthen his trust in God's love in the midst of his own personal crisis point? How might Leon remind the congregation at Leesville Community Church that God's covenant with them is constant as they face the current changes in their community?

Every word of the covenant bears both the function of law and gospel, of confronting us with the terror of our failure and holding before us the promise of grace. Standing in covenant with God is no place for calculations by sharp pencils on finely lined ledger pads. It is a place rather for those who know both the depth of their need and the richness of God's mercy. Leon's awareness of both his human need and God's divine mercy could provide strength in this difficult time. Knowing that God's love and faithfulness are as steadfast as creation might help him to take the risks necessary for change and growth.

To tell the story is to discern when to proclaim law and when to proclaim the gospel to the people of God. When Law is experienced there is need of a gospel word. In darkness there is the need for the proclamation of Light. For example, the most pastoral response to a family at the time of the death of a loved one is to proclaim the gospel word of hope in God's eternal presence and love. The experience of the law is already painfully known in death and in the physical presence of the coffin.[72]

The minister serving as priest in the roles of proclaimer and teacher is challenged to balance law and gospel. The law, understood in a functional sense, exposes our brokenness and sin. The law forces us to encounter our failure and finitude. Law is whatever it is that confronts us with our utter creatureliness in the face of the creator. To reflect on the law is to reflect on the need for God's grace or the gospel word that brings healing and bridges the estrangement from God, self, or others.

As proclaimer and teacher how can Leon hold out both law and gospel to the people in his congregation? What is the law message in the church situation? Where is the gospel message needed for healing? In Leon's *personal* situation what is the proclamation of the law? Of the gospel? To serve faithfully as teacher Leon must live out what he teaches. In order to have credibility with the community Leon must find a way to embrace God's word of law and grace for his own life.

Walking the Line

The priestly role as line judge requires the identification and maintenance of the boundaries of the community, and therefore a keen sense of boundaries. As things in Leesville change, boundaries between pastor and parishoner as well as between parishoner and parishoner are all the more important, but all the more in danger of being crossed. When people are scared and in darkness it is harder for them to identify and maintain boundaries. Fear has a way of blurring boundaries. The need for personal fulfillment can blind an individual from seeing the needs of another or the needs of the greater community.

In times of darkness and fear it is vital for the leader of the community to serve as a source of direction and healing. A skilled and strong leader can name the boundary issues and model clear boundaries for the sake of the whole community. This modeling is especially important for those who have been hurt and are vulnerable to confusion around boundaries.

It is not surprising that a pastor would be sought out to help in the healing of crossed boundaries. It is also not surprising that, at the time someone is seeking help, the pastor might be at a particularly vulnerable point in his or her personal or vocational life. At present, Pastor Leon is in vocational turmoil as well as personal stress. The community's primary boundary keeper is in danger of losing the integrity of his own personal boundaries. He is confused about where exactly those boundaries are and need to be. This is a time when a group of peers to provide support and a mental health professional for his own therapy work would be helpful. Such a professional could also provide consultation and supervision of his counseling situations.

To clear up any possible confusion during times of personal vulnerability, some denominations have set forth policies and procedures for ministers to follow as they fulfill their responsibilities.[73] Sheryl C. Fancher of the Midwest Career Development Services, Kansas City office, said:

> Religious bodies must develop professional guidelines that clarify roles, boundaries and behavior. These guidelines could be as specific as establishing set limits on time, place and circumstance of pastoral visits and counseling sessions. Most pastors have little knowledge of behavioral therapies. They need established relationships with professional psychologists and counselors for referral. They need to identify signs of over-involvement with a parishoner. To maintain accountability they need to enter into a covenant with another minister or professional counselor for supervision. A pastor must also build boundaries around family and private life. Limiting time and job demands could decrease some of the stress factors that lead to greater vulnerability.[74]

There was a time when one of the characteristics that distinguished pastoral ministry from other helping professions was the relatively unrestricted relationship between pastor and parishoner with fluid boundaries. While a physician or attorney or professional counselor would typically see patients/clients in a formal office setting by appointment only, a pastor and parishioners had access to each other pretty much any time, anywhere. Not only that, but a minister's access and availability was not limited to times of ill health or specific problems, but extended over the entire life cycle. A pastor was usually a most welcome visitor in the maternity ward and at the funeral home, and just about anytime in between!

The times have changed. While there are many pastors and parishioners who still relate to each other in much the same way as they used to, it is caring and prudent for the sake of ministry to consider what might today be appropriate boundaries to maintain in pastoral care and counseling situations. Additional suggestions and guidelines for the parish minister in regard to pastoral counseling are included in the Appendix, "A Word about Pastoral Counseling: The Who, What, Where, When, and How."

Why more attention to boundary issues? Boundaries do not need to be established because ministers are less trustworthy than they used to be. The vast majority of pastors and other religious leaders are ethical and committed persons doing their best to answer God's call to ministry. Rather, more attention to boundaries is necessary in light of the heightened public consciousness of clergy abuse. It is wise to avoid even the appearance of any impropriety that might raise mistrust of the pastoral leadership, which would hinder ministry to the congregation and be harmful to the pastor as person.

A second reason for ministers to identify potential boundary issues and concerns is to be better able to respond appropriately in pastoral care situations. There are some boundary concerns for ministers to consider in light of what is being learned about sexual abuse. In advocacy roles, listening to victim-survivors, we have learned that sexual abuse is experienced as a violent violation of all aspects of personhood. The individual's physical, emotional, mental, and social being is deeply traumatized, as is their spiritual core. Such boundary violations tear at the foundation of trust in relationships. The power differential between a pastor and a parishoner in need of care creates a relationship in which there is vulnerability by nature. For the victim-survivor of previous abuse, this can be especially frightening.

Given the violating impact of sexual abuse, it is imperative that clear and safe boundaries are set and maintained. For example, a pastor's casual touch or friendly hug intended to convey care and warmth may be experienced by the one receiving the touch or hug as being disrespectful, invasive, and threatening. Our good intentions are irrelevant to how the receiver will experience our touch. Marie Fortune writes, "The toucher may intend the touch to convey a certain kind of message (support, affection, etc.); but the message is entirely dependent on how the receiver perceives the touch, and the toucher has no control over this."[75]

There are many factors that are involved in the experience of the receiver, such as the receiver's current emotional state and life situation, and the receiver's feelings about and experiences with touch, which may include a possible history of abuse.

We do not know who may be healing from, or even may now be experiencing, an abusive relationship. Because uninvited physical contact may not be perceived as genuine caring, it is wise for pastors to respect personal boundaries and, as a general guideline, not touch or hug without clear invitation. Then, if there is an invitation to greet by a friendly hug or casual touch and the pastor also feels comfortable with such a greeting, an appropriate expression of caring may be shared.

Honoring boundaries of one who has experienced the violation of boundaries and subsequent disregard for personhood, is one of the best ways to convey the intended care and warmth. Such pastoral care is a gift of healing to the victim-survivor of sexual abuse because it affirms an individual's right to choose when and how to be approached.[76]

For ministers who have been violated themselves, ministering to victim/survivors of sexual, physical, or emotional abuse can be especially challenging. Again, a caring peer group for support can be a helpful tool for self-care. Professional counseling for the minister may also be healing and the appropriate place to deal with personal issues. In ministering to victim-survivors, it is also helpful to remember that the victim-survivor's situation, pain, and experience is not your situation, pain, and experience. Keeping your experience separate from the victim-survivor's experience enables you to be more of the help you want to be.[77]

Along with supervision, regular personal counseling or consultation with a therapist can also be a context within which a minister can recognize any personal vulnerabilities that might affect pastoral care and counseling with those in their care. Rather than seeing personal counseling as a sign of weakness, the strong minister understands that all human beings see only in part. A trusted counselor, especially one who really understands the challenges of the ministry and ministers, can be of invaluable assistance as we seek to provide effective ministry through faithful self-care.

Sometimes something will occur during a pastoral counseling session that is troubling to the minister. The parishoner may make a remark that could have a double meaning, or there may be an expression of romantic interest in the minister, or physical behavior such as an uninvited hug or kiss. Of course, it is wise for a minister to realize that such things happen and know in advance what to say or what to do that will protect the dignity of the parishoner while maintaining appropriate boundaries. If a minister has regular supervision or counseling, it would be well to have an immediate review of what occurred along with suggestions for how to most caringly handle the next pastoral contact with that parishoner. Even better, it would be helpful to discuss with the supervisor or counselor in advance of such challenging situations what could be caring, pastoral responses that are least likely to embarrass the parishoner and still protect the pastoral relationship. How could this kind of discussion in advance be helpful to Pastor Leon when Flo asked him to "stop by after work for dessert and a great liqueur that goes with it?"

We can see how carefully situations must be discerned in order to find the greatest good for the community of God. Pastor Leon has a particular choice before him to make. He can use his authority and power as a minister to protect Flo at this vulnerable time in her life, or exercise a power over her by neglecting his responsibility to use the power of his role in behalf of those he serves. A further understanding of the dynamics of power that exists in our covenant relationship follows.

8

COVENANT *&* POWER

POWER AND POWERLESSNESS
"I Just Can't Wait to Be King"

U sually seminarians just can't wait until graduation and ordination! In denominations that have a lengthy period of preparation, students who begin preparation for ministry immediately after high school may have seven or eight years of college and seminary ahead. In many seminaries, about half of all students are second career, which means seminary comes later in life. The waiting to become a leader in the church can seem long, indeed.

Disney's movie *The Lion King* had a scene in which young Simba looked over what would one day be his domain. As he surveyed all that his eyes were able to see, he broke into song, "I Just Can't Wait to Be King!" An important part of his education was learning from his Lion King father, Mufasa, that being the King of Beasts did not mean having power over others, but rather power *with* and power *for* others. The greater the power, the greater the responsibility.

Most seminarians and active ministers understand responsibility. Faithful ministers do not become ministers to lord it over people, but because the Lord has called them to serve others. Very frequently, rather than feeling powerful, ministers may feel quite powerless. Ministers rely on volunteers. Ministers can invite and encourage individuals and groups to offer their time, talent, and treasure, but there is really no way to *make* people respond.

Seminarians who become ministers may be surprised by their inability to make things happen. One of the major mistakes those new to ministry make is to try to force a change upon a congregation for which the congregation is not ready. Changes in worship patterns are among those most likely to meet with resistance. Changes in the way that decisions are made is also likely to disempower some while empowering others, and so patterns of decision-making may be another area where parishoners are resistant to change. Idealistic seminarians bring with them a clear notion of how things should be. If change is imposed on a congregation, the seminarian may be shocked by the reaction.

Ministers also may have problems with power dynamics. First, anyone new to a parish is well advised for at least six months to a year not to initiate significant changes. The early months of a new ministry need to be a time of listening to the congregation, a time to learn their history, and a time to let the congregation know they are loved. Leadership that does not clearly come out of care for the members of a congregation is more likely to be considered suspect as to motivation and resisted.

A second situation that can activate power dynamics is when a congregation is moving, using Rothauge's categories, from a patriarchal to a pastoral church, which is more pastor-centered. Even more so, the movement from a pastoral to a program church is apt to meet with resistance. This time, though, both laity and the pastor may resist the change, because both are losing a valued way of ministering together. The pastor is not able to do as much personal ministry and, from the parishioner's perspective, the ministry received from the pastor is often not as personal as it was before the church became larger.

Where Do I Stand?

There are additional factors that enter into the feeling of powerlessness that some ministers feel today. Ministry for centuries has been an honored vocation. Usually, ministers occupied a position of trust in the communities they served. Ministers were considered professional persons and often regarded even more highly than persons from other professional walks of life.

Today, some ministers do not like to think of themselves as professionals. They seem to be concerned that the word "professional" depreciates the ministry as a calling, a vocation oriented not to professional privilege but to servanthood.

Unfortunately, there are those in the community who also have questions about the professionalism of ministers, but for radically different reasons. Scandals in recent years have occurred so frequently and have been so highly publicized that the public response to a minister is no longer automatically one of respect. As we noted in chapter 7, the community typically understands the word "professional" to be positive, associated with advanced education, high ethical standards, and the provision of a service at a greater level of competency and care than could reasonably be expected from a non-professional. When pastors not only preach about the seven deadly sins, but are perceived to be about as likely as anybody else to practice them, the community may no longer assume that a minister will be trustworthy just by virtue of the fact that the minister is a minister.

Furthermore, there is a tendency in a secular, achievement-oriented business environment for ministers to be seen by some lay leaders as employees of a congregation. This perception is very different from a theology that believes that the minister is really not even called by the congregation, but by God, to lead the congregation. With an employee mentality, the minister may be relegated to take care of spiritual things, while the real business (and power) belongs to the lay leadership.

"Where do I stand?" is an honest question that a minister may have. Far from feeling powerful, a minister may feel quite helpless and vulnerable. This feeling of powerlessness may actually contribute to a minister somehow rationalizing behavior that is clearly inappropriate and inconsistent. Yet, the reality is that the power in the minister's role does not depend on the minister's *feeling* of power, but on the power of God. The minister as a representative person carries in the office of the ministry the power of the sacred. When the minister is someone's pastor, power is inevitably present, whether the pastor feels powerful or not. And with that power comes responsibility.

The Power of Predecessors

Finally, a part of the power dynamic that ministers may face has to do with the power of predecessors in the parish. That power can come in various forms. The most obvious is when a minister enters a congregation after a congregation has been led for many years by a beloved pastor. There are inevitable comparisons. The power of the former pastor can be almost palpable at times. If the former pastor has died, and the spouse remains as a member of the parish, there is also an ongoing visible reminder of what has been lost that can be difficult for some. At times, supporters of the previous pastor may feel they would be disloyal to their former pastor if they rallied too enthusiastically behind their new minister. If there is no intentional interim period filled by an interim pastor following a long pastorate, the next minister who is called by the congregation may find it impossible to remain very long, thereby becoming an unintentional interim pastor.

Power dynamics also appear after previous pastorates that may not have lasted a long time, nor been as highly regarded. A ministry may have terminated in a traumatic leadership crisis through malfeasance, misconduct, autocratic behavior, incompetence, and the like. Whatever the cause, if it is extreme in one direction or the other, and traumatic for the members, that termination is likely to leave a residue of fears that will affect how trusting the members will be of the new minister. Rather than assuming that the new minister will be a person of good will, competence, and caring, members may be wary and trust may be hard to achieve or very tentative.

Sometimes the power of the predecessor is related to nothing that unusual, but simply to personality differences between the former pastor and the new minister. In *God's Gifted People*, sixteen personality types are discussed.[78] These sixteen types can also be sorted into the distinctly different gifts of practicality, personal helpfulness, possibilities for people, and the gift of looking ahead. A former pastor with the gift of practicality would be experienced quite differently from a new minister who leads with the gift of possibilities, for whom practicality is not a high priority. Or, the former pastor may have been always ready to respond with a personal helping hand in times of trouble. The new minister may be wonderful with long-range planning and developing programs for community social action, but not have a gift for one-on-one pastoral care and support. The priorities of the new minister may be hard for members to appreciate if they had come to value the personal support of the former pastor.

The power of the predecessor can continue through nostalgia for what was, or through fear that what happened could happen again, or through a deeply felt personal preference for one form of ministry over another, as well as in other ways. A new minister who does not understand the congregation's experience with previous pastors will probably wonder why leadership seems to be such an uphill battle and why there are negative reactions when the minister does things that worked quite well elsewhere.

Those who "just can't wait to be king" often find that being in a position of power is quite different from what had been anticipated. On the other hand, those who focus not on the power but on the responsibility of leadership will find in the Old Testament additional perspective on what covenantal leadership actually entails.

THE MINISTER/PASTOR AS KING

The Hebrew term for king, *melek,* is most likely related to the Akkadian term *malaku,* which means counsel, advise. The *melek* or king was one whose office and rule was characterized by wise counsel.

The king in Israel was capable of acting imperiously. One need think only of King Rehoboam, for example, who angered the people of Israel with the threat that, rather than with the whips that his father, Solomon, had disciplined them, he would discipline them with scorpions (1 Kings 12:11). In fact, the Deuteronomistic history is thoroughly shaped by an anti-royalist sentiment which regards the king as liable to the worst sort of abuses.[79] The Deuteronomist blamed the apostasy of King Jeroboam and the treachery of King Manasseh for almost single-handedly bringing about the destruction and ruination of the northern kingdom of Israel by Assyria and the southern kingdom of Judah by Babylon (2 Kings 17:21-23; 23:26-27). The reason why the abuses of power were so outrageous was because the king was meant to be so much more.

The King as Inviolable

One of the basic symbols identifying the king in ancient Israel was anointing the king with oil. The verb "anoint" is the Hebrew word *mashach,* which lies behind the noun *meshiach* or messiah.[80]

The action of anointing a king was associated with the king's inviolability. God's favor resides with special protective grace upon God's anointed (Ps. 2:2; 18:50; 20:6; 28:8). Recall David's concern that no harm come to Saul because Saul was the Lord's anointed (1 Sam. 24:6-10; 26:9-11, 23). The warning issued in Ps. 105:15, "Do not touch my anointed ones" (cf. 1 Chr. 16:22) is echoed by the prohibition against cursing the anointed (2 Sam 19:21; cf. Deut. 22:28). The above laws only make sense in a context in which the king, far from being considered virtually inviolable, was in reality thought of as eminently vulnerable to physical attack. Because of the king's obvious and extreme vulnerability, he was anointed in order to provide a symbolic sense of relief from their deepest fear.

To speak of the anointed, then, is to speak of one who more than any one else symbolizes the vulnerability of the community, but yet at the same time, and precisely because of this radical vulnerability, symbolizes the special protection promised by God. Like God's anointed, the church has from its inception had a keen awareness of its radical vulnerability in the face of persecution and disdain. But it has also had an equally radical awareness of divine protection that would sustain it in the midst of its most fearful trials. "The gates of Hell shall not prevail against it," we are promised (Matt. 16:18). We are keenly aware of the fragile nature of our faith and of the precarious situation in which our congregations often find themselves. The pastor is a constant reminder before the people that we cannot take our faith and our futures for granted, but that everything rests in the protective care of God, who has anointed us in our baptism.

The King as Shepherd

One of the oldest and most commonly found metaphors used for kings in the ancient Near East was that of the king as shepherd. Hammurabi of ancient Babylon, for example, referred to himself as the shepherd of his people in the prologue to his famous law code. Following in this long tradition, Israel too referred to its own king as its ro`eh, its shepherd. It is this metaphor that lies behind the symbolic shepherd's staff held by the bishop in the bishop's office of oversight. Originally this office of oversight, or episcope, was associated with every priest.

The metaphor of the shepherd is a troublesome one, however, because it presumes that those for whom the pastor is accountable are like sheep with little ability to take responsibility on their own. When viewed from this perspective it is appropriate to be wary of the implications such a shepherd metaphor has for the exercise of public ministry. However, the shepherd metaphor is not intended to describe what the sheep are like. It is intended to tell us only what the responsibility of the shepherd is. What ought to be equally troubling is the potential abuse to which such shepherding lends itself. Some of the most stirring prophetic judgment oracles are spoken against Israel's shepherds who have scattered God's flock and have not attended to them (Jer. 23:1-4), or who are concerned not with feeding the flock but with feeding themselves, while the sheep are preyed upon by wild animals (Ezek. 34:1-6).

The shepherd not only had to lead the flock safely to fresh pastures. He also had to rescue the flock from danger. The verb for rescue, *natsal*, often connotes the tearing of an animal from the jaws of the beast that is attempting to devour it. Such a job is not a task for timid souls, but rather often requires that the rescuer face into the jaws of the beast itself. But this job also requires perspective and balance, lest the shepherd mistake every moving shadow for the beast. Problems emerge when the pastor is identified principally as a rescuer. When the pastor is a rescuer it sets up a dysfunctional pattern of burnout for the pastor and increases the dependency of a congregation.

It can also lead to harm when ministers in a congregation avoid helping a hurting parishioner out of a concern to not rescue inappropriately. Life experience and professional training equip the pastor to recognize which shadows are ominous and which are safe, which inclinations are deadly and which are benign. There are indeed times when the shepherd must extract the sheep from the mouth of the beast; in times of crisis and deep inner turmoil, when doubt and despair threaten to consume hope; in times of conflict and ill will, when anger and frustration threaten to devour charity and grace; in times of self-confidence and prosperity, when guards are relaxed and the beast has the easiest time of all. The shepherd must have stone and sling at hand.

The King as Guarantor of Justice

Just as the priest was associated with the teaching of Torah, the king was charged with its practical and daily administration. Commonly throughout the ancient Near East the king was considered the person through whom the gods conveyed their eternal laws. More significantly, however, the king was considered the person who symbolized the execution of justice on behalf of the people—and especially those people who were trapped on the margins of the social order. The king was the primary defender of the rights of the widow, the orphan, the sojourner, and those who had no other recourse to social representation. This accounts for the many stories in the Hebrew Scriptures in which a marginalized person goes directly to the king for redress of a grievance. The king was symbolically the guarantor of their justice.

Throughout the ancient Near East, as well as in Israel, the primary criterion by which the king was evaluated was whether or not he was a *melek yashar*, a just king. Kings would often initiate reforms in existing legal codes, grant periodic amnesties, and oversee judicial processes in order to demonstrate their commitment to justice and righteousness. Solomon prayed for a discerning mind that he might justly govern his people, distinguish between good and evil, and discern what is right (Kings 3:1-9). Prayers for the king to be given God's own justice and righteousness were frequently on the lips of those worshipping (Ps. 72:1). The king was understood to be God's regent in the people's midst, responsible to see that God's own justice and righteousness were distributed especially to those who cried out for such justice (Ps. 99:1-4).

For the pastor to embody the metaphor of king among the people means to represent God's justice on behalf of the marginalized and the vulnerable members of our society. The pastor is to embody the church's commitment and passion toward the homeless and landless, those who lack family and social support. The pastor is to be their advocate before the congregation and the wider community, to plead for the equal distribution of justice, to manifest what in liberation theology is referred to as God's preferential option for the poor. The pastor serves the congregation in working for justice on behalf of those who have no voice of their own.

Just as the metaphors of prophet, priest, and king were applied to Jesus as expressive of his ministry among us, so these metaphors have often been applied to leadership within the church. Unfortunately, they are frequently applied in unhelpful ways that do not understand the function of these persons within Israelite society. The prophet was not primarily one who confronted the people with their stubborn rebellion, but one who interceded on behalf of the people's health and well-being. The priest was not primarily concerned with the pedantic performance of right sacrifices, but rather with channeling the holy and life-giving power of God into the life of the community in concrete and usable ways. The king was not primarily concerned with the exercise of sovereign and imperious power, but rather with guaranteeing the principle of distributive justice among the weak and the vulnerable.

These metaphors can be helpful in instructing us as to what leadership among God's people entails, but only if they are correctly understood within Israel's own social context. These chief metaphors invite us to shape our ministries around the same concerns: proclamation of the prophetic word from the vantage of humble intercession before God; celebration at the priestly altar as a tangible means of making God's grace concrete; and administration of the royal court as chief advocate for all who have no other advocate. Proclamation, celebration, and administration—these are the central tasks of ministry in which pastors and other leaders in our congregations are called to lead us in our common ministry.

KINGLY COVENANT-KEEPING
The Strength of Weakness

Pastor Leon is feeling vulnerable in his ministry. He does not like feeling weak, defenseless, and unprotected. From the perspective of kingly covenant-keeping, however, Leon is potentially in a much stronger position than he would be were he to be feeling invulnerable at this time. Because of the vulnerability of the Israelite king, special precautions were taken to assure the king's protection. If the king were thought to have been invulnerable, those precautions would not have been taken and, as a result, the king would have been more at risk. In other words, while vulnerability may be perceived or experienced as a weakness, the awareness of being vulnerable is a strength because it can lead to appropriate safeguards.

In his vulnerability, Pastor Leon needs to take certain precautions. When a person is feeling stressed and stretched beyond personal capacities, self-care and collegial support are all the more essential. If there is a mutual ministry or staff support committee in the congregation, that committee can also assist in identifying appropriate safeguards. The purpose of self-care, collegial, and congregational support, of course, is to take care of the leader for the sake of the people who are dependent on the leadership of the leader. It is not a matter of privilege, but rather of responsibility. The leader is responsible to provide leadership. It is responsible to take whatever precautions may be necessary to make certain that the needed leadership can continue to be provided.

One practical benefit of feeling vulnerable, then, is a greater awareness of the need to keep one's guard up. In addition to self-care and appropriate collegial and other social support, Leon needs to keep in mind that any form of escape from the pressures of his present situation may be especially attractive, and especially risky. Generally speaking, in a time of stress and crisis, major changes or major decisions of any kind are not desirable. They feel desirable, because the change holds the promise of relief from the stress. They are not in fact desirable because the decision is likely to be less well thought through in terms not only of immediate relief but of long-range consequences.

For example, Leon is having questions right now about continuing at the congregation in Leesville. He is also wondering about continuing in pastoral ministry anywhere. If he stays in Leesville, he is wondering about going into a business partnership as a way of bolstering his sagging financial situation. To add to this vocational stress, the health of his marriage and family life are also at risk.

Leon is looking for a way out of the pain that he is in, which is quite understandable. Unfortunately, ways out can be deceptively attractive but filled with hidden perils. In some denominations, resignation from a parish without appropriate consultation and exploration of alternatives may be considered arbitrary and an obstacle to future vocational possibilities within the church. Engagement in a dual relationship with a congregant, such as entering into a business partnership, may be considered by some in the congregation or within the denominational judicatory as a breakdown in pastoral ethics. At the very least, it would be even more painful than the present situation if the business failed and the partners blamed each other for the failure. Any sense of ongoing pastoral relationship would be lost, at least with the business partner, but probably also with the partner's family and friends in the congregation and community.

Another unfortunate decision would be if Pastor Leon were to let his dissatisfaction at home lead him to lean on Flo in a way that is inappropriate for a pastor to relate to a parishioner. As in any other dual relationship, to become dependent on Flo would compromise Pastor Leon's ability to fulfill his responsibility to her as shepherd.

Walking through the Valley

One of the most beloved passages of Scripture is the Twenty-third Psalm, "The LORD is my Shepherd." The psalmist trusts the Shepherd of his soul, fearing no evil even though the psalmist walks through the valley of the shadow of death. It is the presence and care of the Shepherd, the rod and staff used for the protection and benefit of the flock, and the steadfastness of the Shepherd's love that leads to the psalmist's joyful exultation in the Lord.

Trust and trustworthiness characterize the relation of members of the flock and those who represent the Shepherd Lord as ministers of congregations. The members of a congregation need to be able to trust that their minister has their best interests at heart at all times. This is the responsibility that goes along with the power of leadership in the Name of the Good Shepherd.

Whether she recognizes it or not, Flo is vulnerable at this time. The death just two months ago of her father, with whom she had been very close, means that she is still struggling with grief. It would be natural for her to reach out to someone she considers strong and sensitive to her needs. Pastor Leon, as her shepherd, needs to be there for her in her loss, but he cannot allow himself to be a replacement for her loss. That would only complicate the grief process and leave her in a worse place than she is in.

When, through conversation with Flo, Leon began to get in touch with his own feelings of loss, that is a signal that he needs to have someone to talk with, too. But not to Flo. She has not been called to be his shepherd, and such a role reversal would not be in her best interests.

Several factors may cloud Leon's perspective and lead to the possibility of inappropriate action. Leon is anxious about both his life situation and his ministry. He has already experienced some losses, including the loss of self-esteem, and he is anxious about additional losses that may be coming in the near future. Under conditions of anxiety, our vision tends to narrow. The world seems to be collapsing on us. The typical response is to want to run. "The psalmist expressed the existential crisis experiences of the people of God in the metaphor of 'the valley of the shadow of death' . . . As the darkness of the valley closes in, there is a desire to flee from the darkness, to run through the valley. The anxiety of a crisis reduces our life to a valley and propels us to rush through, just as fast as we possibly can."[81]

Flo does not want the pain of bereavement. Leon does not want to endure his personal and vocational pain any longer than absolutely necessary. The human temptation for both Flo and Leon is to want to run through the valley of shadows. They may be tempted to run through the valley together.

But Pastor Leon is the shepherd. The shepherd in the psalm is one who helps the psalmist walk, not run, through the valley. Upon Leon's experiencing his own desire to run through the valley (run from ministry, run from the stresses of home life, run . . .), the appropriate place for Leon to turn is to someone who can be a shepherd for him. That cannot be Flo.

All shepherds need a shepherd. There is nothing wrong with Leon that he is thinking and feeling as he is. Thoughts and feelings are neither right nor wrong, they just are. It is much healthier to be aware of thoughts and feelings, so they can be faced honestly. There is nothing wrong with Leon's needing support. To be a shepherd does not mean always feeling powerful. But it does mean never to use the power of the role in such a way as to negatively affect a member of the flock who is being served. It means not doing anything that might scatter God's flock or being concerned to feed oneself when the flock needs to be fed. It means not being a wolf who looks at the flock hungrily, but rather protects the flock against anything or anyone who would take advantage of the weak. The shepherd is one who uses power with and for the flock.

Community Conscience

The special concern of the anointed shepherd (the called minister) is for those who are most powerless. The king in Israel was the guarantor of justice, with particular concern for those trapped in marginality: the widow, the orphan, the sojourner, and others whose voice in the community was weakest.

Pastor Leon is needed in his congregation and in his community as one who is committed to justice and righteousness. As Solomon did, Leon needs to pray for a discerning mind so he will know what is right and how to most effectively advocate for those in his congregation who have little or no voice of their own.

Leon does not need to deny his own feelings of powerlessness in order to fill his role as advocate for those in special need. On the contrary, his being aware of his own thoughts and feelings during this time can help him identify with those who cry out for relief. The problem arises in over-identification—to the point that it is primarily his own pain that is propelling him and his own survival that is his primary concern. At the point where his focus is on himself rather than on those he serves, he fails in his pastoral responsibility.

Survival in ministry can never be the bottom line for a minister. Christ calls us to be willing to lose our life for the sake of the gospel, to be willing to bear a cross and even to lay down our life if need be in order to save a friend. The enemy of thriving in ministry is to be overly anxious about surviving.[82] To thrive as a covenantal leader, Leon must enter into the uncomfortable place in which many of his members find themselves: on the outside of things, feeling down and out, feeling discouraged, helpless, and, at times, hopeless. As their leader, Leon both identifies with the feelings of those he serves and sees them in need of compassion and God's word of hope.

To lead members of the congregation through the shadowy valley, Pastor Leon does not shirk from embracing the hopelessness many of them feel, and that he may feel at times. Resurrection lies on the other side of dying. Hopelessness can be a place of growth and depth of learning about self: our utter dependence and at the same time our responsibility to make choices that are responsible and life-serving. Pastor Leon's calling through this process is as shepherd and advocate. Always the shepherd, comforting, guiding, supporting, as a word of love. Always willing to speak a word in behalf of those whose voice is unheard, a word of justice.

For Pastor Leon's own sustenance during this difficult time in the life of his parish, there is another word from the Lord. A spiritual benefit of being vulnerable lies in the opposite direction of our strength. The New Testament says it as well as it can be said: "My grace is sufficient for you, for my strength is made perfect in weakness. Most gladly therefore will I rather glory in my infirmities, that the power of Christ may rest upon me" (2 Cor. 12:9).

Ultimately, the shepherd's power does not lie in personal strength, but in the power of Christ. It is in fact when we are not feeling very powerful that God's strength becomes most real to us. Our weakness is God's opportunity. Leon does not have to fear that by entering into his weakness that he will be even less able to lead God's people. It is only as he realizes his personal inability that he will look to God rather than to his own resources. As he lets go and lets God be God, the needed strength is provided.[83] The promise of God that God's grace is sufficient can only be fulfilled at those points where we are radically open and needful. God's strength is made perfect in our weakness, so it is only when we are weak that we are truly strong (2 Cor. 12:10).

This is the mystery of the vocation of ministry. By looking at covenant and work, we can better understand the difference between a calling and a job. We turn now to take a look at how this difference can help sustain Leon during this critical time in his life and vocation.

9

COVENANT & WORK

NOT JUST A JOB
Called to the Ministry

There is an enormous difference between a job and a vocation! An extreme example would be the kind of ministry that is required in the aftermath of a disaster such as a hurricane or flood. If pastors in a disaster area saw parish ministry as a job, what a terrible job it would be! In a disaster, the work hours dramatically increase. Sleep is hard to get, particularly if your own home has been damaged or your own roof has blown away and you are awakened by the flapping of FEMA plastic tarps. Meals are missed and the fast-food places you used to go to before are no longer operating. In the immediate impact and early relief stages, survival is a primary concern and there are many emergent situations. Each time you respond to someone else's difficulties, you may have to leave your own family in equally difficult circumstances. As your adaptive energy dissipates, there is precious little time for rest and renewal. Furthermore, there is no time and a half for overtime, nor any realistic hope for comp time in the foreseeable future.

Yet, pastors who do not see what they are doing as a job but as a calling are sustained during such times by the promise of Christ to be present. Prayers, communications of concern and contributions of sister churches shine through the darkness. Pastors are also sustained by a spirituality that enables them to perceive their situation as David Livingstone did. In *A Personal Reflection*, Livingstone says that:

People talk of the sacrifice that I have made in spending so much of my life in Africa. Can that be called a sacrifice which is simply paid back as a small part of a great debt owing to our God, which we can never repay? Is that a sacrifice? . . . Say rather it is a privilege. . . .[84]

Gifted leaders of the church who serve as bishops and presidents rarely during their tenure look younger than they did when they were elected. Not many get more sleep or wake up less often during the night thinking about a problem situation, not many eat more regularly and nutritionally, nor do many have more time with family and friends, nor do many exercise more regularly and read more books for fun. Not many take more trips where they attend no ecclesiastical meetings and do not talk church. Yet, what is heard from many is not dissatisfaction with a job, but the Spirit-filled contentment of a calling. Those of us who perceive what we do, not as a job, but as a vocation, understand Livingstone when he says, "A sacrifice? Say rather it is a privilege."

However, when things are not going well it is possible for any pastor to lose sight of a call to ministry. Pastor Leon is feeling the stress of increased needs in the congregation due to the economic pressures that many of his people face. Families in his parish need more pastoral care to deal with financial problems and the relational conflicts that arise in a crisis period. Leon is losing sleep thinking about problem situations. With increased work hours it's harder for him to eat balanced meals. The needs in his congregation take him away from the needs of his family, which are equally important. It is no surprise that Pastor Leon wonders: "Maybe I should have stayed in the business world. Do I really belong in parish ministry? Why am I here in this place?" He wonders if someone else could do a better job. No doubt the times have been trying for him and stress has taken its toll. In these discouraging times he questions his call to ministry. He may forget why he felt called to his particular place of ministry and lose sight of the gifts he has to offer there.

But God had a particular reason for calling Leon to Leesville, just as God calls each of us to a particular ministry at a particular time and place. God's call to ministry is still active even at the times when we don't feel very confident about that call. When these doubts and disappointments come, leadership support can be a blessing.

For Leon, leadership support is vital at this time when he is losing sight of his call to ministry. Through a colleague group Leon can find support in being able to faithfully reappraise what is happening in his ministry context so that, in Christ, he can perceive change and conflict not simply as a threat, but as a challenge and an opportunity for mission and ministry.

With the help of colleagues and with eyes of faith we can see ministry as a vocation and not just a job. Our Christian vocation is an expression of our spirituality. We use our gifts for a common purpose, for the equipping of the saints to do the work of ministry and for the upbuilding of the body of Christ. God calls a particular servant with particular gifts to a particular time and place.

How is this call of God discerned and experienced? For a pastor or minister God's call is received through the church. In this way, when the congregation, conference, synod, or diocese extends to the minister an invitation to join them in mutual ministry, they affirm God's call. The "Vision and Expectations" document for ordained ministers in the Evangelical Lutheran Church in America reads:

> (We) believe that the Holy Spirit calls, gathers, enlightens, and sanctifies the whole Christian church. . . . It is the Spirit that provides the church with those persons who are enabled by God to lead the church in carrying out the ministry and mission of the gospel of Jesus Christ.[85]

The call to ministry may also be discerned and experienced through encouragement of our sisters and brothers in Christ as we are affirmed as having gifts for particular ministries. When we are serving in the place we are to be, we are delighted to be there most days. Leon felt called to parish ministry because of his enjoyment and preference for using his particular gifts in the congregation. In fact, the word "vocation" is from the Latin word *vocare*, which means to call. Our vocation refers to the work that God calls us to do.

Open-Ended, Never-Ended

Sometimes our deep gladness and joy of serving are diminished by the stress and strain of daily challenges. Leon is having a difficult time seeing the blessings of ministry. As we have seen, when crisis occurs in the congregation, in the community in which we serve, or in our personal lives the demands on our time and energy increase. Additional tasks and problems are loaded on top of normal activities and responsibilities that are often too much to handle.

Day-to-day ministry involves handling unpredicted emergencies. What is scheduled for the day can change abruptly when ministers become aware of a parishoner in crisis. And when the crisis is addressed the scheduled tasks still need to get done somehow. Interruptions are part of ministry when someone drops by the office or calls and wants to talk. The challenge for the minister is to be as flexible as possible while setting clear boundaries when necessary. The office manager can help facilitate clear boundaries by screening calls and taking detailed messages. Many calls for the pastor are related to products for sale and questions that could be answered by someone other than the minister. Reducing interruptions allows more time for work that the minister is trained and called to do.

At times the work ministers are called and trained to do seems to require more than twenty-four hours a day. An ongoing stress in ministry is not having the luxury of enough time to do our best. The multitude of responsibilities prohibits spending too much time in one particular area of ministry. Some ministers feel ill-prepared going into a Bible study or committee meeting. It is frustrating to know that you have the gifts, the talent, and the skills to do so much better if you could just slow down long enough to use those abilities. For a minister who strives for perfection, doing things halfway is all the more disconcerting. And all the more reason to focus on God's grace to remind us that we do our best in a given situation when we do the best we can, given the resources available to us at the time.

At times the most faithful response when we are overwhelmed with responsibilities and have a full plate already is to say "no." We often try to add just one more thing to our list of commitments. But often that last straw breaks the minister's back! We come face to face with our human limitation. We need to remember at such times that God created us with the need for rest and refreshment. We wisely follow God's commandment to "Remember the Sabbath day and keep it holy." A Sabbath rest helps us offer ourselves in ministry. We provide our best care for the congregation when we respect our limits and renew ourselves in self-caring ways.

The flexibility of ministerial work is often a blessing for several reasons. The absence of a defined schedule outside of meeting and worship times allows ministers to schedule work that requires high energy and focused concentration during the time of day that the minister finds most productive. Flexible working hours also allow for spontaneity when there is an opportunity for self-care or time with family and friends. In addition, with a more open schedule there may be an opportunity for ministers to participate more fully in the care of their children.

Another challenge in ministry is the constant pressure of never finishing or reaching a point where we can feel the satisfaction of completion. Perhaps in a fleeting moment we give a sigh of relief that Sunday's sermon is done but the next moment we are reminded of the sermon we need to prepare for the midweek service. The deadline for the church newsletter rolls around too quickly in the midst of weekly bulletins yet to complete. There is always more to do than is humanly possible.

Pastor Leon finds himself so overwhelmed that the blessings of ministry are overshadowed. Because of the financial problems at church the full-time secretary was cut to part time. This decrease in support staff has increased his workload and his stress. There is less time to prepare for teaching and preaching. In this setting how can Leon feel a sense of accomplishment and success?

What's the Goal?

The blessings of ministry can be overlooked when ministers focus on measuring ministerial success in quantitative terms. When success is defined by the size of a church budget, the number of visitors on a given Sunday, or how many new members joined this year, we fail to recognize the goal of ministry. Jesus calls us to go and make disciples. We succeed each time we tell others the story of God's love. We succeed when we reach out to people in need.

If Pastor Leon defines his success in quantitative terms he will surely feel like a failure. There is a decrease in contributions to the church and they are behind budget. New member classes are down as families are moving out of Leesville to find stable employment.

There is another way to see success besides focusing on numbers and money. For Leon to be successful he only needs to be a faithful servant of God who proclaims the gospel through Word and Sacrament. If he can focus on *this* call and purpose for being at Leesville, Pastor Leon's feelings of failure are less likely to cloud his ministry.

It is said that Christians are called not to be successful but to be faithful. When we are faithful to the covenant God made with us, we are successful in our call to ministry. Reframing success in this way nurtures our gifts for ministry. Out of our faithfulness flows a response of sharing our spiritual gifts for the upbuilding of the community in Christ. Our living becomes our thanksgiving to God.

FAITH AND WORKS

By the design of the creator, our vocational commitments are to be nurtured as we live within covenant relationship with God and community. We trust in God's promise of unconditional love and give of ourselves, not in perfection, but in faithfulness. Being in covenant with God and community relates to living within the context of this covenant relationship. Being right with God correlates to living right with the community of God.

The terms "justification" and "sanctification" have been popularly used to describe this being right and living right. "Faith" and "works" have been used to describe justification and sanctification. Since antiquity there has been a dialectical tension surrounding the discussion of faith and works. In the New Testament Paul preaches justification by grace through faith apart from works while James insists that faith without works is dead.

In sorting out this tension between faith and works, between justification and sanctification, it is helpful to review the biblical understanding of perfection found in the Deuteronomic and Priestly traditions.

Deuteronomic theology placed a strong emphasis upon being thoroughly, even perfectly, obedient to the obligation of living in covenant relationship with God. The demand to choose life or death and to obey God's Torah upon pain of severe judgment is frightening knowing our human frailty and weakness.

To understand what is meant by perfection in Deuteronomic thought several theological convictions must be kept in mind. First, a bold brush is used to paint the portrait of the relatively righteous person, whereas Protestant piety tends to use a very small and detailed brush to illustrate the perfectly righteous person. For example, Luther struggled over his personal righteousness with attention to every detail. Every minor action was an occasion for tremendous guilt and self-condemnation. Every minor blemish stood out in his self-portrait as though it were the focal point of a horrible divine scrutiny. Just as Luther agonized over every mole and wrinkle, every spot and pock mark, we too recognize our essential brokenness and sinfulness. We are hopelessly corrupt, bankrupt before God's judgment throne. The details condemn us.

Deuteronomistic piety, however, did not focus on the details. It was known that if God counted every sin no one would be able to stand. But the focus was not on every detail of human action but rather upon the broad sweep of behavior. To be righteous was not some hopelessly impossible task but was rather thought of as a relative condition in general and broad terms. Psalm 24, for example, lists the conditions for those righteous pilgrims who are qualified to enter the sanctuary: those who have clean hands and pure hearts, who do not lift their souls to what is false, and who do not swear deceitfully. Similarly, Psalm 15 regards as righteous those who walk blamelessly, who do what is right, who speak the truth from their heart, who do not slander, nor do any evil to friends, who take no reproach against their neighbor nor despise the wicked, who honor those who fear God, who stand by their oaths, who do not lend money at interest, and who take no bribe. Such sweeping generalities characterized the manner in which the Deuteronomist tended to think of the righteous life.

This way of regarding personal righteousness is seen in Samuel's claim of innocence as he reviews his life: "Whose ox have I taken? Or whose donkey have I taken? Or whom have I defrauded? Whom have I oppressed? Or from whose hand have I taken a bribe to blind my eyes with it? You have not found anything in my hand" (1 Sam. 12:3-5). The dominant piety of the psalter actually dares to invite divine scrutiny of one's life. The plea for God to test and try the heart to see that indeed the psalmist's heart is pure (e.g., Ps. 17:1-3; 26:2-3; 139:23-24) seems like prideful contempt if not blasphemy. But because the Deuteronomist used a broad brush to paint a portrait of the relatively righteous individual, such an invitation was not a statement of prideful contempt but rather a faithful laying-claim to the divine commitment promised in relationship with God.

The second characteristic of the Deuteronomic counsel of perfection was its conviction that the stipulations of Israel's Torah were doable. Living the faithful life was not some grand impossible test or setup for failure.

Israel's Torah was not so unreachably lofty nor so remote and foreign to human nature as to be impractical. Rather, it was within the human heart; it was immediately accessible and totally within the realm of human capability (Deut. 30:11-14). Living faithfully within the obligation of God's covenant relationship was not only possible but even natural for those with the divine Torah in their hearts.

The third characteristic, however, follows quickly upon the second. As natural as such obedience ought to have been, Israel was doomed from the beginning to failure. But not because of the impossibility of the task nor because of some divine plot to force Israel into failure for a greater goal. Rather, Israel would fail because of its unnatural inclination toward disobedience. The prophets often focused upon how unnatural Israel's disobedience was. Nature in general, and animals of various shapes and stripes in particular, logically know how to behave. But Israel seemed to have this unnatural urge toward disobedience (Jer. 2:11, 32; 8:7; 18:14-16). We tend to regard failure to keep Torah as a natural consequence of our human nature and faithfulness to God's covenant obligation as unnatural. Israel, however, considered it the opposite. Obedience ought to have been natural, and disobedience was outrageously against all the evidences of nature itself.

The fourth and final characteristic of the Deuteronomic counsel of perfection is perhaps most fundamental. The entire concept of Israel's covenant with God was established not as a result of Israel's achievement but as a free gift of God predicated upon the promise made by God with Israel's ancestors. It was not based upon Israel's righteousness or uprightness of heart, stature, or prestige. Indeed, God established relationship with Israel in spite of Israel's insignificance and rebellious nature (Deut. 7:7-8; 9:4-7).

The Deuteronomic understanding of living in covenant relationship is a complicated one, because it is both optimistic and pessimistic. Law and gospel are held in tension. The Deuteronomist rejoiced in God's grace that established the natural and doable relationship, but also understood the unnatural inclination in the human heart toward disobedience and failure.

According to the Deuteronomic way of viewing things, Israel's holiness precedes its obedience. When Israel was chosen by God as a special possession the Lord established Israel as a holy people (Deut. 7:6; 14:2, 21, 26:19, 28:9). In Jeremiah 2:3 the assumption is an a priori conviction that Israel was holy to the Lord. Because of this given and non-negotiable status of holiness, Deuteronomy calls upon Israel to be obedient.

In the Priestly tradition, the relationship between obedience and holiness is reversed. The Priestly tradition calls upon Israel to be a holy nation (Exod. 19:6). Holiness is not something conferred upon Israel from the beginning. Instead, it is something that Israel is called to become in its life together under God. Israel is admonished to "be holy as God is holy" (Lev. 11:44f.; 19:2 20:7, 26). In the Priestly tradition holiness is not to be assumed but is to be worked out in covenant with God.

When the Priestly tradition calls upon Israel to be holy, it is not calling upon the people to be nice or loving. Holiness (*qodesh*) was the life-giving but yet potentially lethal and contaminating presence of the numinous that was symbolized by the temple in the midst of the people. To be holy meant to be cut off from the realm of the mundane or common sphere in which normal life was conducted and to be swept up in the lethal presence of the divine. The call to be a holy people was not so much a moral summons to righteous behavior as it was a cultic summons to mediate and serve as a conduit for God's lethal love on behalf of the world.

For Deuteronomy, holiness was the status into which Israel was called, whereas for the Priestly tradition, holiness was yet to be established as the people lived out the covenant. Deuteronomy considered righteous behavior as doable because of Israel's status as a holy people, while the Priestly tradition considered righteous behavior as outside the realm of Israel's potential. From the beginning of God's covenant, established during Israel's sojourn in Egypt, Israel was incapable of obedience. (Exod. 6:2-4). Ezekiel 20 echoes with the refrain: "But they rebelled against me . . . Then I thought I would pour out my wrath upon them . . . But I acted for the sake of my name" (vv. 8-9;13-14;21-22).

The Priestly tradition presents us with a dramatically different understanding of the relationship of sanctification and justification than does Deuteronomy, both in the way it regards sanctification, meaning Israel's holiness, and the way it understands the relationship of such sanctification to obedience. For Deuteronomy, Israel's holiness is the essential precondition for its call to obedience. For the Priestly tradition, God's gracious forgiveness based upon the integrity of the divine holy name is the precondition for Israel becoming a holy people, and this occurs apart from "works of the law."

The concept of covenant is understood in Deuteronomy as contractual;

two consenting parties agree to certain conditions in exchange for mutual commitments. This is symbolized by the central iconograph of the ark of the covenant that holds the two stone treaty documents outlining the obligations. In contrast, the Priestly tradition shows the ark not as a container for the treaty stipulations but rather the footstool representing the divine presence. The Priestly tradition shifts the thought away from a contractual relationship based upon the conditions of treaty obligation to a non-contractual relationship based solely upon the abiding presence of the holy one. Holiness is not something one gains by doing. It is rather Israel's way of being in relationship with the nations of the world and with the cosmos itself.

The Israelite viewed ethics and cultic purity as integrally related. Ethics and purity are corollaries of one another just as sanctification and justification are equivalent terms. Sanctification and justification relate to two different perspectives upon reality. Sanctification is the cultic/ritual term that expresses the restoration of nature's wholeness and the healing of nature's demise due to the incursion of primal chaos and anti-orderliness. Justification is the corresponding forensic term that expresses the ethical restoration from violence and injustice and the healing of history's demise due to human sinfulness.

According to the Deuteronomic view, we *are* God's holy people by virtue of being set apart, just as the holy things were set apart for the priest. We are God's special possession, made holy by being brought by God into relationship with the divine. Within the context of this sanctified relationship, which is a non-negotiable given, we are encouraged to choose life. According to the Priestly view, within the context of God's eternal covenant (from which the element of human initiative has been removed) we are nevertheless to be God's holy people because God is holy. We *are* God's sanctified people (Deuteronomic), and we are *invited to be* God's sanctified people (Priestly). Being who we are and becoming by doing are not mutually exclusive. We are God's sanctified people, and we are called to be God's sanctified people. Both are true. It is when we stress one over the other that we get trapped into legalism (with its stress on what we do) or antinomianism (with its stress on who we are).

Similarly, concerns for sanctification and justification can't be played off against one another, some saying, "I'm justified, so I don't need sanctification," and others saying, "I'm a holy person, so what's to justify?" We experience brokenness both in the ordering of the universe around us, the context in which we lead our lives (nature) as well as in the historical sequence of our actions (history). To experience the restoration of the cosmos that surrounds us and that provides the context for our daily living relates to what the biblical witness considers sanctification. To experience the restoration of the brokenness of our history, corporate and private, and the disruption caused by human action in history relates to what the biblical witness considers justification.

Faith and works are not opposites. To have to choose for either faith or works, either justification or sanctification, would be fundamentally unbiblical. Justification by grace frees us to believe. And we are sanctified through the Word of God and the sacraments of Holy Baptism and Holy Communion. Day by day God makes of us a new creation, a new person in Christ. We are always in the process of becoming, much like the saying, "Please be patient, God isn't finished with me yet!" Martin Luther wrote:

> This life therefore is not righteousness but growth in righteousness, not health but healing, not being but becoming, not rest but exercise. We are not yet what we shall be but we are growing toward it, the process is not yet finished but it is going on, this is not the end but it is the road. All does not yet gleam in glory but all is being purified.[86]

All we are and all we do is set within the context of God's grace. God does not abandon us because of imperfection. God is with us. Not only our gifts, but even our imperfections can be used for God's glory. Luther understood that we cannot by our own understanding or effort believe in Jesus Christ. By the Holy Spirit, we are called through the gospel, enlightened with spiritual gifts, sanctified and kept in true faith.[87] Justified and sanctified we respond to God's grace. We give thanks through works of love and by keeping promises in our covenant relationships.

COVENANT AND PROMISE-KEEPING
Spiritual Promises

All of our covenant relationships, including the vocational and personal promises we courageously make and strive to keep, rest on God's promise of unconditional love and abundant grace. God's spiritual promises are woven into the very nature of who we are and are as close to us as the air we breathe.

The Israelites believed God's covenant of unconditional love to be as certain as the stars in the sky and the fish in the sea. God's love is constant. As suggested above, God's covenant is made not simply with Abraham and Sarah, or Moses or David, or even with the people of Israel, but rather with all of creation. Recall once again how the prophet Hosea thinks of God making this covenant "with wild animals, the birds of the air, and the creeping thing of the ground." The rainbow is a sign of this everlasting covenant between God and every living creature of all flesh that is upon the earth (Gen. 9:16). This universal covenant of God with all of life rests not on creation's doing but on God's call of that creation into being.

In the beginning the Spirit of God moved over the waters. The Word of God called into being light and firmament; dry land and vegetation; the moon, sun, and stars; birds and fishes; animals and humanity. All that God created and blessed came alive through the breath of the Spirit. The Hebrew word for "breath" is the same word for "spirit," God's *ruah*. The Spirit or breath of God that moved over the waters stirs within all that lives. By creation we are spirit-filled or spiritual beings. We don't have to do anything to make God's Spirit reside within us. God's Spirit is part of who we are. We simply need to be.

The presence of God is as near to us as our breath. Job said that he would not speak falsehood as long as his breath was in him and the spirit of God was in his nostrils (27:3). In troubled times it can be comforting and calming to meditate on God's promise of presence as we center on our breathing in and out. We receive a "new breath" in meditation and prayer, according to Henri Nouwen, who said that "prayer is God's breathing in us, by which we become part of the intimacy of God's inner life, and by which we are born anew."[88] This is similar to what Paul wrote to the Romans about the Spirit helping us in our weakness to know how to pray as the Spirit intercedes for us with sighs too deep for words (8:26).

God's covenant with us is always a promise of relationship, a promise of unconditional love and ongoing presence. God promises, "I will live in them and move among them, and I will be their God and they shall be my people" (2 Cor. 6:16).

Communion with the Divine is offered; the promise of "being known and knowing, being loved and loving." What is given in this covenant is

God's word backed by mighty deeds shown throughout history: "Off-spring are conceived in old women; slaves are liberated from hopeless bondage; people lost and wandering in a desert are finally led home; one who dies is raised from the dead."[89] God is the trustworthy and faithful promise keeper.

God promises to embrace us as we embrace one another in relationship. Walter Wangerin Jr. speaks of God's continual presence in the union of marriage:

> God embraces in (God's) own knowing the present and the future together: God who is here with us now, as we begin the relationship, is also, right now, at every anniversary of that relationship until we die. God is at the birthing of any children we may have, blessing the event. God is at the tragedies that may come. God is supporting and consoling us there now, even as (God) stands here smiling upon our promises. Therefore, we can go forward trustingly, even to the difficulties, because God joins the times for us. God comforts and enables us despite our ignorance—to trust in (God) who knows the future as good as though we knew the future ourselves.[90]

In the Great Commission in the Gospel of Matthew, Jesus commands his disciples to "go and make disciples." The charge is to teach and baptize those who have not heard the good news, just as the unchurched need to hear the message today. Jürgen Moltmann is quoted as saying, "*promissio* involves *missio.*"[91] The promise received brings with it a mission . . . the healing of the world with special attention to the outcast, the widow, the orphan, the sinner. Jesus sends the disciples out with the power of the gospel for the work of justice. In faithfulness to the covenant they have known in Christ, the disciples love as they have been loved.

The command is accompanied by a promise. The disciples are not abandoned by Jesus, left to carry out this mission on their own. "I am with you always" is the promise. On the night of his last supper with his disciples Jesus promised that the Holy Spirit, a Counselor, would dwell with them forever so they need not be afraid. Jesus gives them peace to calm their troubled hearts. Jesus promises to prepare a place for them so that they can join him in heaven after their mission on earth is done. Their abiding with Christ has no end.

Vocational Promises

It is God's covenant with us that sustains our vocational promises. God calls us and provides for our ministry. God's covenant with Abraham and Sarah upheld them as by faith they obeyed God's call to go out to a place that they were to receive as an inheritance. They went out, not knowing where they were going, knowing only that God would provide. Both Abraham and Sarah counted on God's faithfulness to the covenant. Abraham and Sarah believed God the promise maker to be God the promise keeper. And God reckoned it as righteousness.

But when we experience insecurity about our gifts and sense of call it is often hard to trust in the promise keeper to provide for us in ministry. When called by God we may respond not with self-confidence like the prophet Isaiah saying, "Yes, Lord, here I am, send me," but, like Leon, out of a sense of self-doubt and with protest. We would not be the first to protest God's call. We are in good company with saints that have gone before us, like Moses, Jeremiah, Mary, and Jonah. Many great leaders of the faith felt inadequate to serve.

Moses protested repeatedly: Who am I that I should go to Pharaoh and bring the people of Israel out of Egypt? They will not believe me. I am not eloquent. I pray God, please send some other person! Each time Moses raises an objection to why he can't serve, God provides a way for him to overcome his expressed feeling of inadequacy. God promises to be present with Moses and equips him with the mighty power of God—power that can turn a rod cast to the ground into a serpent and can cover Moses' hand with leprosy and restore it back to healthy flesh again. When Moses expresses doubt about his ability to speak, God promises to be his mouth and teach him what to say. God even provides the support of Moses' brother, Aaron, so that Moses does not stand alone.

Jeremiah also protests that he does not know how to speak. He feels that he is too young to be a prophet. But the Lord's touch on Jeremiah's lips provides the words. And then there is Jonah. When the Lord directs him to Nineveh, Jonah protests. Nineveh? Why me, God? Why Nineveh? However reluctantly, Jonah follows God's leading to Nineveh and serves with the knowledge of God's mercy and steadfast love.

Even Mary, the mother of our Lord, wonders why she is chosen to bear the Savior. When the angel brings God's message that the Lord is with her she considers what sort of message this might be! She has no husband. She has not known a man in order that she might conceive. But the angel tells her that with God nothing will be impossible, that she need not be afraid because God will provide. Mary sings praises to God and rejoices in the Lord's mercy and justice. Once regarded as a handmaiden in low estate, now Mary will be blessed by all generations.

When God calls us for ministry, God provides for us. Resources may come from unexpected places but all that is needed will be given. God says: I'll take you just as you are . . . I'll equip you and be near you. We may voice all sorts of protestations and face many obstacles and challenges during our ministry, but we are never alone in the serving. With God nothing is impossible.

The only way we can make a vocational promise is with the help of God. In one denomination's service for ordination, the ordinand is questioned: "Before almighty God, to whom you must give account, and in the presence of this congregation, I ask: Will you assume this office, believing that the church's call is God's call to the ministry of Word and Sacrament?" The ordinand responds, "I will, and I ask God to help me." When entrusted to preach and teach in accordance with the Holy Scriptures and the creeds and confessions she or he promises, "I will, and I ask God to help me."[92] Two more times this promise is spoken as the new pastor vows to study the scripture, to pray for God's people, to nourish them with the Word and Holy Sacraments, to lead in faithful service and holy living, and be a faithful witness of God's love. The presiding minister acknowledges that it is the almighty and gracious God that gives the will to do these things and the strength and compassion to perform them.

A stole is given as a sign of the work of ministry and the yoke of Jesus that restores the minister as Jesus promised. When we labor and are heavy laden, Jesus provides rest for our souls. We learn from Jesus who is gentle and lowly in heart, for his yoke is easy and the burden light (Matt. 11:28-30).

The newly ordained is addressed, "Tend the flock of God that is your charge, not by constraint but willingly, not for shameful gain but eagerly, not as domineering over those you charge but being examples to the flock" (1 Pet. 5:2-3). God provides us with authority and power to be the trustworthy shepherd of our flock. The charge is to use our authority for the flock's protection and edification in a power with, instead of a power over, model of ministry.

The promises have been spoken. The stole has been given. The clergy gathered in partnership for the gospel have offered their blessings in the laying on of hands. The exhortation is given, "Be of good courage, for God has called you, and your labor in the Lord is not in vain."[93] The ordained kneels to receive a blessing, and the assembled people of God call upon the Divine to equip the pastor with everything good so that God's will is done.

God helps us make and keep our vocational promises through providing us with many blessings. The company of other believers is part of this equipping. The ministry of the church is a mutual ministry. Pastor Leon is in ministry *with* his people, not over and against, in a shared partnership for the sake of the gospel. The pastor is not the only one who makes promises in the service for ordination. The congregation speaks on behalf of the whole church, receiving the ordained as a messenger and servant of Jesus Christ. They promise to pray for and honor the ordained in support of his or her work of ministry over the days to come. The gathered people promise to in all things strive to live together in the peace and unity in Christ. The ordination is not complete without the promises of the Body of Christ. Through their promises, joined with the promises of the ordained, God creates the relationship of mutual ministry.[94]

Personal Promises

The vocational promises we make are connected to our personal promises because our ministry is a calling and not just a job. We are ministers at all times, not just when we are wearing our collars or vestments and not just when we are preaching or teaching or visiting with a parishoner. Our pastoral identity does not depend on performing a ministerial function at a given time, but rather on the promises we made at our ordination to be faithful servants of Christ. The "Vision and Expectations" document for ordained ministers in the Evangelical Lutheran Church in America further outlines what is required of ministers if they are to be faithful examples of service and holy living. The ELCA affirms that our witness to the gospel not only depends on what we do but on who we are.

It is impossible to disconnect our vocational promises from our personal promises. The keeping of our vocational promises will be affected by the keeping or breaking of our personal promises. How we conduct ourselves in our families, in our relationships, and in our communities can either diminish or strengthen our ability to give faithful witness to the gospel. Through our devotion to our personal commitments we honor

God and what God has created. Think of how devastating it would be not only to Pastor Leon's marriage but also to his vocation for Leon to involve himself in a romantic relationship with a parishoner. In addition, how would going into business with a parishioner affect Leon's ability to keep his vocational promises to the congregation?

In the "Vision and Expectations" document the ELCA encourages clergy to practice spiritual discipline and healthy self-care for the good of the whole church. Participation in the means of grace through the renewal of baptismal grace in individual confession and absolution, receiving the sacrament of Holy Communion, and quiet time for prayer and Bible study are ways to receive God's "renewing, sustaining, empowering Spirit both personally and in the practice of ministry."[95] Pastors are encouraged to be an example of holy living and self-care through proper nutrition, exercise, and recreation. When there is evidence of physical or mental illness, substance abuse, eating disorders, or relational problems, consultation with a professional is recommended.

In addition, the ELCA expects ministers to work in a collegial relationship with one another and to be mutually accountable while respecting those in positions of leadership and oversight in the church. Support through regular contact with colleagues and judicatories is part of intentional self-care as well as the keeping of vocational promises. Leon's ministerial colleagues could be instrumental in helping Pastor Leon see which choices would be the most faithful in his work and personal life.

The minister is responsible to see that his or her life does not become "an impediment to the hearing of the gospel or a scandal to the community of faith." Three areas of concern are: responsibility to family; separation, divorce, and remarriage; and sexual conduct. Whether married or single, ordained ministers are to uphold a biblical understanding of marriage in their public ministry as well as in their private life. Family members are to be regarded with love, respect, and commitment with expressions of forgiveness, reconciliation, healing, and mutual care.

The biblical witness is that commitment in marriage is to be inviolate until death. When human brokenness tests this commitment, marital counseling is encouraged. If reconciliation is not possible and divorce is sought, the synodical bishop is to provide guidance. If a minister decides to marry following a divorce, the counsel of the synodical bishop is also recommended.

The minister recognizes that human sexuality is a gift of God that is to be honored. The covenant of faithfulness to vocation and to family rejects sexual manipulation, abuse, and promiscuity. The ELCA document reads, "Single ordained ministers are expected to live a chaste life. Married ordained ministers are expected to live in fidelity to their spouses, giving expression to sexual intimacy within a marriage relationship that is mutual, chaste, and faithful."[96]

Marie Fortune devotes an entire chapter to "Faithfulness" in her book, *Love Does No Harm.* She states that, "Faithfulness can be fulfilled through truthfulness, promise keeping, attention, and the absence of violence."[97] Promise keeping is part of our commitment to another person. "Promises are the particulars of a relationship, the things that matter, the things that two people need to hash out and come to some agreement about if they are to fulfill their responsibility of faithfulness to each other." Relationships are set in the context of the community that provides support, a reality check, encouragement, affirmation, and, when necessary, challenge.

In our discussion of vocational promises, we have seen how the community of the assembled people of God participate in the promise-making. Both the ordained and the congregation make promises in the presence of God and representatives of the church, thereby giving their word of faithfulness. The community takes part in sustaining the relationship through its faithful support of the covenant.

Our personal promises may also be witnessed by the community. The covenant that begins the marriage between a bride and groom is witnessed by family and friends who, by their presence, pledge their support in the days and months to come. They become part of the fabric that holds the two promise makers accountable to their word. Once again, as with ordination vows, the assembled people of God provide a context for the union of two parties. The community who gathered to witness the promises provides vital stability when the stress of daily life threatens the keeping of those promises.

Marriages cannot survive for a lifetime based on feelings of love. Margaret A. Farley, author of *Personal Commitments: Beginning, Keeping, Changing*, states, "Feelings are occurrences that happen to (or in) us. They come and go; they are like (and they include) physiological sensations . . . Love is not feeling, and our commitment to love cannot reasonably be a commitment to feeling."[98] About commitment Farley says: "We give our word of commitment and in doing so we give a part of ourselves; we place something that belongs to us into another person's keeping. The root meaning of commitment lies in the Latin word *mittere,* which means to send. When we make a commitment we send our word into another; we dwell in the other by means of our word. Because of the nature of commitment, Farley states, "We always stand to lose a part of ourselves if we betray that word."[99] Since breaking a commitment is also a loss for the person who breaks it, we see how keeping a promise not only cares for the other but also cares for the self. To follow through with a commitment is to uphold the integrity of our word; it is to uphold an integral part of our very being.

Margaret Farley also observes that our commitment to love seeks to safeguard us against our own inconsistencies; it is love's way of being whole while it still grows into wholeness. It is the recalling and remembering of the covenant that sustains the couple during the difficult times. Walt Wangerin, writer and theologian, believes that "until death parts us" has the faithfulness of the Divine.[100] It makes a home for the vulnerable, worried heart. It is this promise of faithfulness, of being there for each other for whatever is to come, that provides a context of safety and security for working out a resolution to conflict. The promise facilitates trust, essential for the renegotiation of the relationship throughout the cycles of life. Through a lifetime of changes the covenant remains timeless. For Leon and Leah, the covenant promise of marriage can serve as a bridge during the difficulty in their present situation until easier times come.

The Divine intention is for all relationships to be life-giving, for promises to be kept, for the covenant of marriage to be a lifelong commitment, for parents and children to stay together in the same household, and for friendships to be joyful blessings. God empowers us to choose life in all we say and do. To be faithful in our relationships, our decisions to choose life for ourselves also means that we make decisions that are also life-serving for the people we love. We make these life choices not out of obligation but in thankfulness to our creator. Hence, Farley reflects, "Faith can serve to free us from a compulsive sense of obligation; it offers us hope in forgiveness, or liberation from too narrow a view of our options. It can summon us to courage, to brave patience or bold action, to faithfulness that could be, but somehow is not, beyond our strength."[101]

Jesus goes beyond the legal and moral obligations and asks us to do what is life-giving in our commitments—for our spouse, our friends and

COVENANT AND WORK 125

family, all our beloved. And in order to help us discern what is life-giving, Jesus provides us with guidelines such as love one another as I have loved you, and love your neighbor as yourself. Jesus also identifies hedges to alert us that we are approaching a boundary so that we can prevent a boundary violation. For instance, Jesus expands the meaning of the commandment "Thou shalt not kill," saying that our anger and insult can be just as destructive. "Thou shalt not commit adultery" is broadened by Jesus to include looking at another with lust in your heart. Jesus cautions us to guard our healthy God-given sexual desire so that greed and lust do not take over love. The feeling of lust is the hedge that, if taken seriously, alerts to the possibility of crossing a boundary. Becoming aware of the hedge therefore provides an opportunity to reconsider what choosing life means in that particular situation.

God intended only wholeness in relationships. But what happens when promises are broken? When the covenant cannot be sustained even with the help of friends and family who witnessed the promise making? What are we to do when "until death do us part" becomes "until the death of the marriage parts us" and the death of the marriage occurs before physical death? What happens when people who began marriage with the under-standing of a sacred life-long union now find that their relationship has disintegrated to harmful interactions? What happens when friends who once shared themselves so freely discover that trust has been broken beyond mending?

We enter covenants with promises of love but God's love is the only constant, perfect love. Some relationships end. Some friends grow apart. Some marriages fail. Part of our brokenness is that it is not always healthy for a covenant to be kept. Sometimes, after all resources have been utilized, the healthiest choice is to acknowledge the death of the relationship. Sometimes the life-giving choice is to forgive, to heal, and to go on.

When we are in that painful place of a broken covenant and a broken heart, ministers need to rely on friends and resources outside of the con-gregation. From time to time each of us find ourselves trying to navigate turbulent waters in our relationships. Every human union contends with elements of brokenness and failure.

But God provides for us in the midst of imperfection, failure, and bro-kenness. We have received forgiveness in our risen Jesus Christ who renews our covenant with God when we fail. We often begin our worship acknowledging that we are in constant need of God's absolution. Only then can we offer forgiveness to one another. Only then can we share the peace of God and Holy Communion with one another as the united body of Christ.

God calls us as a community to choose life. Choosing life means protecting and nurturing the promises we make. God calls us to encourage one another to remain faithful to our covenants even in difficult times. God calls us to learn with one another how to forgive and be forgiven. We live out our commitments keeping in mind that all the promises we make, whether they are in our vocational or personal lives, are supported by God's first covenant with us.

With the changes taking place in his congregation and at home, Pastor Leon is having trouble keeping his vocational and personal promises. In the midst of Leon's imperfection, failure, and brokenness, he is in need of hearing *God's* promises, the gospel word of God's love and grace, and the promise of strength sufficient in time of need. How will God fulfill those promises for Leon?

10

COVENANTAL LIFE

A KNOCK ON THE DOOR
At the Boundary

Remember the quandary Pastor Leon was in when Flo called him in his office? It has been a particularly stressful day. The offering receipts for the month had been the lowest so far, and the treasurer told Leon that he will have to make a very pessimistic report at the council meeting tomorrow. Leah has to work tonight, so at least he won't have to deal with her reaction to the congregation's falling finances and the implications for their household.

As Leon sat in his office wondering what to do, the telephone rang. It was Flo. "Oh, Pastor Leon," she said, "I'm so glad you're there. I'm feeling a little down. Maybe you remember that tomorrow would have been my father's birthday and I'm going to drive over to see Mom. I was wondering if you could come by tonight to give me some ideas about how to support Mom tomorrow—that is, if you don't have to work. To thank you, I made something special for dessert and I just discovered a great liqueur that goes with it."

Leon doesn't have a meeting. He takes a deep breath. "Ahhhh," he said, "I . . ." Just then there was a knock on Leon's office door. "Can you hold for just a minute, Flo," Leon continued. "Someone is at my door." "Sure," Flo replied, "but I hope you'll be able to come by."

Leon pressed the hold button, let out the breath that he realized he had also been holding, and walked to the door just as he heard a second knock and a woman's voice say, "Leon, are you there?" Leon opened the door and to his surprise it was his colleague pastor, María. María looked distraught.

"What's wrong," Leon asked. María took his arm and said, "I really need to talk with you. I've got a problem."

"Of course," Leon said, his brow wrinkling in concern. "Oh, just a minute. I've got a call on hold."

Leon walked over to his desk and reached across to the telephone. Activating the phone again, he said, "Flo, something's come up that I have to take care of right now. I don't know how long it'll take. I'll have to get back to you. Is that OK?" "Well," Flo said with the slightest of sighs, "I hope it won't take *too* long. I'll be here waiting for your call."

Leon swallowed once, hard, said "Goodbye," and hung up the telephone.

He turned to María. "Here, come sit down," Leon said. "Tell me what happened."

María looked at him, tears welling up in her eyes. "I think I'm in trouble," she said. "I don't know what to do."

"I'll do whatever I can to help," Leon assured her. Quietly, he sat near her, angling his chair so he could see her a little better.

"I can't believe what just happened," María said. "I was at the church when Juan came by, you know, my committee chairman. I thought he wanted to talk about the Board meeting, but he didn't. He wanted to talk about his feelings for me. I knew he liked me, but not like that. I didn't know what to say. He's a nice person and I don't want to hurt his feelings, but I don't know about getting involved with someone in the congregation. The part that really got to me is I realized when he was talking how lonely I am and I really didn't want to send him away."

"How did you leave it with him?" Leon asked.

"I thanked him for sharing his feelings with me," María said, "and I told him I'd have to think about what he said. Then I lied a little and said I had to make a hospital call. Juan wanted a hug before he left and I felt myself stiffening a little when we did, then he left. I just don't know. . . ." María's voice trailed off.

"What bothered you most about what happened was . . . ?" Leon deliberately left the question open ended. "My vulnerability," María half whispered. "I'm afraid I could cross a boundary and I don't want to do that."

Boundaries as Blessings

Leon and María talked for a long time, especially after Leon told María about the telephone conversation he was just having with Flo and how he was feeling at the moment the call was interrupted by María's knock on the door.

Their conversation had two parts, not by design, but just because it happened that way. First they shared for some time much more than they ever had before about how badly they had been feeling. Both were experiencing more isolation and pain in their ministries than they could easily bear. In addition, the losses were mounting. Neither was as confident or hopeful now, as ministers or as persons, as they had been when they came to Leesville. Self-esteem had also plummeted.

Both pastors felt lonely, although their life situations were very different. Leon's loneliness was the kind that can occur in the midst of a family when the family no longer seems to have a common purpose and when they are not there to support each other. María's divorce had not separated her from her grown children and grandchildren, but she had no comforter at home for her when she finished a long day. Which was the more lonely feeling neither Leon nor María could say, but they agreed that it wasn't a good feeling for either of them.

Both acknowledged being sexually vulnerable right now. Leon told María about his estrangement from his wife. "When Flo called and invited me over tonight, I was seriously tempted to say 'Yes.' Then you arrived. Providential," Leon said, pursing his mouth and letting his breath out slowly. Leon's "Providential" was expressed as half-question, half-exclamation!

"Yes," María agreed, "just like you're being here at the office later today than I thought you would be."

The second part of their conversation was about what boundaries are appropriate in ministry. María was especially helpful since she seemed to have a clearer idea of where those boundaries were and why they were important to respect. Her divorce had been very painful and she had learned a lot about herself in the counseling that followed. Growing up, her grandfather had been jovial, except when he had been drinking. Then he turned mean and abusive. María saw what her grandmother endured. When she became old enough to overcome her own fear and angrily protest what she saw, her grandfather turned on her. Later in her own marriage, she did not have to put up with drinking, but her husband had one affair after another. The crossing of boundaries by two very significant men in her life and her feelings about them took a long time to overcome in therapy. She acknowledged that right after her divorce she tried to deal with her feelings of rejection and loss by finding a sympathetic male. She realized after a short time that it was not the other man she wanted, but relief from her pain. When in seminary she was taught about appropriate boundaries in ministry, she intuitively understood that the existence of boundaries was a blessing rather than a burden. She had committed herself always to honor those boundaries. It wasn't until Juan approached her that she had ever felt in danger of crossing one. She knew that she could not remain Juan's pastor if their relationship took a turn in the direction that Juan was suggesting.

Leon listened carefully to what María was saying. As for his own situation, Leon was a good man and intended to harm no one. It had simply escaped him that his relationship with Flo was cozying into a comfortability that Flo's grief and his loneliness could convert into a compromising situation. María's reminiscences helped Leon understand that as the shepherd, it was his responsibility to keep the flock from harm, most of all a member who was already hurting and having a hard time dealing with a loss.

Beyond the Boundaries

The blessing of a boundary is that it protects a relationship, as we noted in chapter 7, making that relationship safe by an uncompromising commitment to the well-being of the other. In a minister-congregational member relationship, there may be times when a member tests that boundary or indirectly or even directly challenges the need for the boundary to exist. In a pastoral relationship, the existence of a sexual or other significant ethical boundary is always a blessing if the pastoral relationship is to be maintained. The crossing or breaking of that boundary will inevitably result in the loss of the pastoral relationship.

It is not for fear of consequences that boundaries are maintained by ministers, although serious consequences usually follow. Rather, it is because the minister is called to be a blessing and wants to be faithful to that call that most ministers, like Leon, quickly re-establish any boundary that is in danger of bending, as was his with Flo. María, too, listened to herself as she confided in Leon and, also through Leon's honest communication, resolved that she wanted to maintain only a pastoral relationship with Juan. They shared ideas as to what each might say so that the pastoral relationship would be maintained, but without insulting or depreciating or rejecting Flo and Juan as persons.

Beyond the boundaries within which ministers must live and work, though, there is the very real question of how to deal in healthy ways with the pressures of ministry, and the temptations that sometimes arise, as they have with Pastor Leon. Before we review specific answers to that question, we turn once again to the spiritual foundation on which any answer must rest.

TO BE, TO DO, TO SEE

One of the primary expectations that parishioners have of their ministers is that they be persons of spiritual maturity.[102] What does spiritual maturity look like? How might spirituality be expressed in the day-to-day life of those who lead God's people?

To fully ground and integrate ministerial health and wellness issues in Christian spirituality, we need to look at two of the crucial components of spirituality. One has to do with who we are, the other with what we do. Then we'll take a look at what may lie closer to the heart of spirituality— how we see.

Spirituality as Being

Who are we as Christians? Identity questions are crucial to a minister's self-understanding as a Christian. The witness of Scripture is clear. Christian identity is grounded in the grace of God in Christ Jesus. Systematic theologian T. A. Kantonen summarized the theological reflections of St. Augustine, Luther, and Kierkegaard as "Christocentric existentialism."[103] Our very life flows from God the creator, who made us the way we are as embodied, thinking, feeling, and relating beings. A Christian spirituality does not split off spirituality from the four dimensions of our humanness—the physical, mental, emotional, and social—the flesh and blood reality of creation.

As we have seen earlier, the physical, mental, emotional, and social dimensions of who we are interrelate and interact. What significantly affects us in any one of those dimensions will affect each of the other three as well. When Pastor Leon's body is hurting from overextension or illness or lack of sleep or poor nutrition or lack of exercise, he also thinks less clearly, is less emotionally sensitive to the needs of others, and does not relate at his best. Similarly, when a person is deeply troubled in mind, perhaps having lost a sense of possibilities and vocation, that person's mental anguish will be reflected in feelings such as depression, in disrupted interpersonal relationships and, if the stress goes on for some time, perhaps the stress may also be reflected in the development of physical symptoms.

When something significantly affects a Christian as a physical, mental, emotional, and social being, God-questions are raised. When things go wrong with our bodies or with our primary relationships, we ask "Why, God?" We may not actually say God's name, but, whether spoken or unspoken, Christians who believe that God is omnipotent and loving will always want to know where God is when bad things happen. Spiritual integration of a loss is not complete until a Christian has some way of understanding the who, what, where, when, and why of God in relation to that loss. Our faith is not that God will rescue us from all the bad things that may happen to us, but that we can count on God to be present when they do. Spirituality as a hoping mechanism is grounded in the confidence that who we are is an outgrowth of whose we are, and that nothing can separate us from the love of God in Christ Jesus.[104]

Who are we? The Christian response is that we are God's children, justified by the grace of God through faith in Christ Jesus, spiritually centered not on ourselves but on the Word of God. We are utterly dependent on the grace of God in Christ Jesus, and our faith is that God's grace is sufficient. Ralph W. Sockman put it this way when he wrote *The Meaning of Suffering*:

> Our Christian faith holds that this universe can best be explained as the creation of an Almighty God whose . . . nature is revealed in the life and love of Jesus Christ. Resting in this undergirding faith, we confront all problems. . . . In whatever happens, we have faith that God is working for our best interests. This kind of trust helps to change the mental outlook in ways that aid the healing process . . . the defeatist spirit is lifted to new hope; the weary mind finds new strength; the burden of guilt is removed by the assurance of forgiveness—all this is

of immeasurable aid in opening the way for God's healing work. . . . And even if our (problem) is not cured, we discover with St. Paul, when his thorn remained, that grace is given sufficient to bear it. . . .

—2 Corinthians 12:9[105]

Spirituality as Doing

Another common answer to the question, "What is spirituality?" focuses not on who we are (our being) but on what we do (our doing). This component of spirituality is troublesome to those who want to be careful not to misidentify spiritual life as some kind of a necessary way to God. An evangelical theology maintains that no human way to God is needed because God has come to us and provided a way for us through Christ Jesus. The evangelical emphasis on God's initiative is underscored by a confession of our human inability even to know God, let alone come to God, without our first being called, gathered, and enlightened by the Holy Spirit.[106]

Yet, spirituality, however evangelically well-defined, is incomplete unless it is expressed. That is why a discussion of vocation is often included in efforts to describe spirituality.[107] A sense of calling in daily life gives expression to a relationship with a God who gifts us in differing ways. Scripture speaks of the importance of Christians using these gifts on a day-to-day basis for the common good and the upbuilding of the body of Christ (Eph. 4, Rom. 12, and 1 Cor. 12). Gifts are to be used not as though we possess the gifts, but as those who are good stewards of the varying gifts of God. As stewards, our responsibility is to help those people who receive our services see *through* what we give in service *to the Giver*, as God ministers through us (1 Pet. 4).

Doing is not opposed to evangelical theology. In *the Book of Concord*, Martin Luther says:

It is also taught among us that good works should and must be done, not that we are to rely on them to earn grace, but that we may do God's will and glorify (God). It is always faith alone that apprehends grace and forgiveness of sin. When through faith the Holy Spirit is given, the heart is moved to do good works.[108]

The regular exercise of spiritual disciplines, such as Bible study and prayer, is an expression of spirituality. Spiritual disciplines are not a way to God, but they are among the ways that Christians over the centuries have said "thank you" to God.

Spirituality as Seeing

Along with defining spirituality in terms of being who we are and in terms of doing a discipline to express our thanks to God, spirituality can also be defined, as we suggested in chapter 5, as a way of perceiving, a "seeing with the eyes of faith."

Fifteen years ago, studies of pastors and spouses showed that when change is perceived less as a threat than as a challenge, when a person experiences a sense of having choices, and when Christ is perceived as a very real presence in stressful times, the subjective feeling of stress and anxiety is significantly lower.[109] In addition, Christians who positively (faithfully) reappraise what is going on in their lives also practice significantly higher levels of self-care and spiritual discipline. As noted in chapter 5, this way of approaching problems by seeing them through the eyes of faith was called faith-hardiness. A hopeful and hardy faith is not something that a person develops by willpower, because it is not a person's own power that makes the difference. It is a faithful trusting in the God who promises to be with us during the darkest times, even as we walk through the valley of the shadow of death. It is trust that the God who promises will faithfully keep those promises. If the burden were on our faithfulness in keeping our promises, sooner or later every one of us would fail to measure up. An evangelical spirituality does not rely on our ability to keep our commitments. When we think of promise keeping, we look not to ourselves but to God. The cross of Christ is a sign of how far God is willing to go as a promise keeper.

In chapter 5 we suggested the cruciform character of Ephesians 3:14-19 ("that Christ may dwell in your hearts through faith; that you, being rooted and grounded in love, may have power to comprehend with all the saints what is the breadth and length and height and depth, and to know the love of Christ . . ."). In Greek the word for "comprehend" is *katalabesthai*. *Katalabesthai* comes from a root that in some of its forms can mean "perceive." The Ephesians verse could then be that we have the power to *perceive* with all the saints the cruciform (height and depth, length and breadth) love of Christ. The cross of Christ is at the heart of our spirituality, and through the cross we are able to see the love of God.[110]

Ephesians 3:14-19 immediately precedes the Pauline emphasis in Ephesians 4:1-6 on our unity (one Lord, one faith, one baptism, one God and Father of us all, who is above all, and through all, and in all). Then, in Ephesians 4:7ff, the Pauline message emphasizes our diversity through our being differently gifted. Spirituality *as a way of seeing* makes it possible to see through all the diversity of gender, age, race, and culture to our oneness in Christ. Spirituality as a way of seeing enables us to see Christ even in the least of our sisters and brothers. Spirituality *as a way of seeing* also helps us recognize in our differences the marvelous gifting of God, who asks not that we all be the same, but that we all express our spirituality by using our gifts for a common purpose, the equipping of the saints for the work of ministry, for the upbuilding of the body of Christ.

Growth in spirituality means more than having occasional workshops on spiritual disciplines, although that may be very helpful. Growth in spirituality also must be understood as related to a faithful way of seeing. Persons in ministry need support in being able to faithfully reappraise what is happening in their ministry contexts so that, in Christ, they can perceive change and conflict not simply as a threat, but as a challenge and an opportunity for mission and ministry.

COVENANTS AND CARE

Knowing the Gift

A major ministry of the church is to help women and men and children to see their God-given gifts. Once identified, the biblical charge of the church is to equip God's people to use their gifts for the upbuilding of the Body of Christ (Eph. 4:12). This discerning of gifts is crucial as the church seeks out or responds to those who believe themselves to be called to full-time ministry.[111]

The gift passages of the Bible identify God's gifts as including certain roles, such as apostle, prophet, evangelist, pastor, and teacher (Eph. 4). If the gift passages stopped there, a lot of God's people would not feel gifted, for relatively few fill such roles. Fortunately, the Pauline letter to the Ephesians is complemented by Paul's letter to the Romans. In Romans 12, Paul also makes reference to gifts that include roles, but are not limited by them.

For example, he speaks of evangelism and teaching, but also of service and giving aid and doing acts of mercy, functions that can be contributed by Christians whether or not they have an official role in the church other than as a member of a congregation.

What is not as commonly considered is that the gift passages of the Bible include more than the gifts of role or functions. Psalm 139 suggests that an even more foundational gift is the gift of personhood.[112] Who we are is a gift from God, preceding what we later learn to do, or the roles we are later called to fill. Consider some other examples of how *being* precedes *doing*. Moses' experience of God was that God's being (God's "I AM") preceded God's doing (God's deliverance of the Hebrews from Egypt). For Christians, the central gift passage of Scripture is John 3:16, which identifies the God who loves so much that even the Son is given. In the Christian life, baptism, in its infant expression, is clearly linked with being rather than doing. It is not what the infant does (know enough, believe enough, do enough) that is the basis of baptism, but God's love and gracious acceptance of the infant without condition. As the child grows and later becomes mature in the faith, then what the child or adult does can be a way to say "thanks" to God.

Pastor Leon is himself a gift from God, although at times he may not appreciate himself or feel as affirmed as he would like. His giftedness as a person precedes his becoming a pastor. He also has many gifts for ministry, if he has the eyes to see them. The most faithful perception of his gifts will reveal that those gifts are not limited to those things about himself that he sees as strengths. On the contrary, his awareness of his limitations during this time of transition in the life of his congregation and of his family can be a great gift. As we have seen, for him not to perceive these limitations would lead him to overlook his vulnerabilities, rendering him all the more vulnerable.

Pastor María, as a person and as a pastor, is also one of God's gifts. She gifts Leon when she comes to him in her confusion. By bringing to Leon something that so closely mirrors his own dilemma, María gives Leon the opportunity to acknowledge his own vulnerability. If he chose not to share his vulnerability, the opportunity could be lost. To Leon's credit, he accepts the gift María gives by giving the gift of his own honest confession of personal turmoil. The two colleagues then have a chance to be there for each other in a way that can be mutually supportive and faithful to their callings. They have the opportunity together to grow in spirituality, understood as a faithful way of seeing. They can help each other faithfully reappraise what is happening in their ministry contexts and their personal lives. In Christ, they can perceive change and conflict and even confusion not simply as a threat, but as a challenge as a Christian person and an opportunity as pastors for mission and ministry.

Nurturing the Gift

Leon and María, as persons and as pastors, are gifted by God and challenged not only to use, but also to nurture the gifts they have been given. We have emphasized the unselfishness of self-care, since personal gifts cannot be nurtured without faithful self-care.

For church denominational leadership to approach ministerial health and wellness issues from a *spiritual* perspective is to perceive physical, mental, emotional, interpersonal, and vocational issues not as a threat to the effective functioning of ministers, but as a challenge and an opportunity. A focus on health and wellness supports the spiritual growth of our leaders and their families as increasingly good stewards of body, mind, emotions, and relationships. Through this stewardship, ministers have yet another way to say "thank you" to God for the gifts of life and vocation. By encouraging pastors and their families in this stewardship of life, church denominational leaders are also encouraging mission and ministry.

Health is not a capital A answer to life. Only Christ is God's answer to our deepest need. Spiritually aware leaders who witness not only with their words but also with their lives will live not for health alone, but for Christ alone. Ralph W. Sockman wrote in *The Meaning of Suffering*:

> Health of body, is therefore, subordinate to health of spirit. Our primary purpose is not to use God to keep ourselves physically fit, but to use our bodies in order to be spiritually fit. Sometimes our bodily pains help to produce spiritual health. After Paul repeatedly prayed for the cure of his thorn in the flesh, he heard the Lord say to him, "My grace is sufficient for you, for my power is made perfect in weakness" (2 Cor. 12:9).[113]

Yet, physical, mental, and emotional health as vigor and strength for life and preparedness for devotion and sacrifice all the better equips pastors and other full-time church leaders for our vocation of "equipping the saints for the work of ministry, for the upbuilding of the body of Christ" and for our mission to go and teach and baptize in the name of the Father, and of the Son, and of the Holy Spirit. Faithful ministers live not for health. Ministers routinely will enter contagion wards to administer the sacraments. Those ministering in areas of natural or other disasters do everything possible to reach missing members. But, when faithfulness does not require otherwise, ministers who live healthily are good stewards of the gift of life and use their health for the sake of Christian ministry and Christ's mission.

In addition to paying attention to his health as a whole person (body, mind, feeling, personal and vocational relationships), for Pastor Leon to nurture his gift will require him to be willing to take a look at his situation from another perspective. Since how we perceive a situation determines our reaction to that situation, Leon perceiving his personal and pastoral situation as threatening will inevitably lead to anxiety and psychophysiological reactions of various kinds. A faith-hardy perspective transforms a previously threatening situation into a non-threatening event.

Spirituality is at the heart of this transformation, because the faith-hardy way of seeing sees the presence and care of Christ in the midst of life's messes. When Christ is present, then there is always hope. There may also be burdens to bear, but even then Christ's promise is that we are not alone. Because God is faithful, we will not be tempted or tested beyond our ability to endure (1 Cor. 10:13).

Practically speaking, Leon and María may need to take turns reassuring each other about God's promises and about God's faithfulness as a promise keeper. At times all of us have problems seeing how God is present and we tend to miss signs of hope that another faithful set of eyes may be able to perceive. We truly need each other. Nowhere is this more true than our need to listen carefully when a ministerial colleague sees something differently than we do. It is not a matter of right or wrong. Rather, the difference in perspective, if not lightly dismissed, may provide an angle of vision that otherwise would escape us. Sometimes just the slightest shift in the direction of that difference may open up a whole new world of possibilities for us. Those who try to go it alone, as Pastor

Leon has for too long, may overlook the challenge because the perceived threat is overwhelming.

María's willingness to self-disclose was the breakthrough. Had she not taken that step, Leon may have taken another unfortunate step in a direction that would have compromised his ministry and his life. From a theological perspective, María's arrival was providential. We never know when we reach out to another person for help if we were led to do so only for ourself, or if our reaching out might also make a significant difference to the other person as well. María received the support she needed, but she then became a godsend to Leon at a potential turning point in his life. Reaching out to a colleague in ministry may therefore not only nurture the gift of the one who reaches out, but also be nurturing in ways that could not have been imagined for the one who responds.

Giving the Gift

Pastor Leon and Pastor María are called not only to nurture their gifts, but to give them. The effective and faithful giving of our gifts is a lifelong challenge. Depending on what is happening in our lives, we may be more or less effective in the use of our gifts. Sometimes we know the way to solve a problem, but our sense of timing is wrong. We offer a solution more quickly than the one we are trying to help is able to hear it. Accumulated experience may help us time our responses more appropriately, with the result that our help is more effective and faithful to our call to be supportive to those who need our support.

When Pastor María came to his door to seek his collegial support, it became clear to Pastor Leon that how María handled her situation with the lay leader could make or break her ministry at her congregation. Only through María's sharing did he begin to see that the way he was responding to Flo was also blurring the boundary between minister and parishioner in a way that could lead to harm for Flo and for himself as a person and pastor.

Not only that, but Pastor Leon began to see that Flo's reaching out to him was not as personal as it may have appeared, but a way to recapture something of what she had lost through the death of her father. Rather than respond to Flo's initiatives inappropriately in the role of a romantic partner, Leon began to reflect on how he could better respond in his role as her pastor. Pastor Leon turned the corner and began to give the gifts for ministry that he had been given even more effectively and faithfully, because he more clearly saw what could only make things worse for Flo and what was truly needed by her in her bereavement.

The story of Pastor Leon is not over with his recognition of how to be a faithful pastor for Flo. The problems in the congregation are not ones that can easily be overcome. Leon's problems at home will also take time to work through. What is crucial, however, is the direction Leon is facing. He was looking only in the direction where hope had taken a holiday. He is now beginning to see some things a little differently. When ministers begin to realize that there are alternatives and options, the awareness of having choices and the significance of choosing life becomes more apparent. Leon is beginning to look in the direction of choosing life.

For Leon, and for all ministers who struggle along life's way, personally or vocationally or both, there is a prayer that has come to mean a great deal to those who are more aware of the journey than they are confident that they know exactly how things will turn out.

> Oh, Lord, you have called your servants to ventures of which we cannot see the ending, by paths as yet untrodden, through perils unknown. Give us faith to go out with good courage, not knowing where we go, but only that your hand is leading us and your love supporting us, through Christ our Lord.[114]

The prayer does not presume faith sufficient for the journey. The prayer request is *for* faith. It takes faith to go where we do not know, to walk an unfamiliar path, to be confident when perils impede our progress that we are being led and loved. We ask for faith to go out with good courage.

Let us pray regularly for such faith, not only for ourselves, but also for all our colleagues in ministry who share our calling to ventures of which we cannot see the ending. The ventures may involve cross-bearing times, defined by Paul Scherer as times when we "try with all (our) might, and have nothing . . . but a hurt for (our) trying, and a heart that keeps stretching anyway as far as (our) arms can reach."[115] Yes, we may encounter the cross along the way. But, thanks be to God, where there is a cross, there is always our Christ.

APPENDIX

THE PARISH MINISTER
AND PASTORAL COUNSELING

Probably the most sensitive area with the greatest risk for boundary crossing is in pastoral counseling by the parish minister. There are even some who suggest that ministers should limit their counseling activity to crisis situations and pre-marital preparation. While all pastors are expected to provide at least some level of pastoral care (individual or relational or congregational support during difficult times), pastoral counseling involves a different set of skills that usually require professional training beyond what is provided in a seminary. For membership at the Fellow level, the American Association of Pastoral Counselors requires an advanced degree in pastoral counseling, to have done at least 1,000 hours of pastoral counseling while receiving at least 125 hours of interdisciplinary supervision in addition to that required for Member/Member Associate levels (a total of 1,375 hours of counseling and 250 of supervision), and to give evidence of an understanding of the counseling and psychotherapeutic process while integrating one's professional role and personal identity.

Since counseling is not as fundamental to the pastoral role as is pastoral care (many very effective ministers do not feel adequately trained to do any counseling at all), some further suggest that any counseling beyond supportive pastoral care needs to be referred.

There are some factors to consider as we try to reduce any sense of boundary crossing in our pastoral care activities. It is helpful to keep in mind that there is no way to guarantee that a specific intended behavior on our part will always be perceived in the way that we intend it to be seen and interpreted.

If assistance is given to an individual or couple in need, it might be wise to limit the number of meetings to three or four and refer any individual or couple that seems to need additional or specialized counseling to professional counselors in the community. The rationale for this approach is to avoid the kind of dependencies and transferences that more in-depth counseling could stimulate. The dependency could result in a counselee looking to the minister to fulfill needs that can only appropriately be filled by someone other than the minister (a spouse, a friend, etc.). Transference is a technical term that grows out of psychoanalytic understandings, but, simply put, it involves a counselee transferring to a therapist thoughts and feelings that go beyond what the therapist is thinking or feeling. Counter-tansference can also take place, where the therapist transfers thoughts and feelings to the counselee that have more to do with the therapist than with the counselee. Reacting (overreacting) to an older person who is not authoritarian as if that older person were your authoritarian mother or father would be a typical example of a transference reaction. Sexual feelings can also be the result of transference or countertransference. When a counseling relationship extends for many weeks or months, transference may be harder to manage. Most ministers are not trained to handle transference phenomena, and so the wiser part of pastoral care may be for the parish minister to not enter into lengthy counseling, since that requires therapeutic skills beyond what a typical seminary provides.

Furthermore, there are some who question whether or not a person who is someone's minister can also be that person's therapist. As a minister, it is necessary to work with people on committees, to supervise teachers and staff, to work through difficult problems on church councils and boards where there may be differences of opinion that have to be expressed honestly, etc. Therapy often involves very personal exploration at very deep levels. A counselee can feel extremely vulnerable as a result of so much uncovering. Consider the problems of a minister seeing someone in extended pastoral counseling or therapy with whom it is also necessary for that pastor to relate as a supervisor or authority figure, perhaps even critiquing the ideas or work of the counselee because of the other roles the minister must fill. While ministry involves a variety of roles, relating to a parishoner as both a minister and a therapist is a dual relationship that is problematic. The pastoral counseling relationship, except for crisis or short-term counseling, is one that has a high potential for compromising the pastor's ministry by the development of a destructive dual relationship and/or by involving the pastor beyond the scope of seminary training. Even for trained pastoral counselors a foundational premise of the code of ethics for the AAPC is "To diagnose or provide treatment only for those problems or issues that are within the reasonable boundaries of our competence."

Even in crisis or short-term pastoral care and counseling it is helpful to guard against the possibility of misperception or misinterpretation of otherwise innocent behavior. Newspaper writers are used to getting the facts by asking questions about the *who, what, where, when,* and *how.* That newspaper framework will assist us in raising the relevant boundary issues.

The *who* of pastoral care and counseling reminds us that, first and foremost, the minister is a minister. The primary role of the minister as pastor or teacher or leader must never be compromised by the pastoral counseling role. If compromise could occur, then referral is the most faithful action to take. The minister, of course, responds to crisis situations regardless of who in the congregation is in crisis. But even in such crisis situations when we must respond to a house call, if there is a high potential for the blurring of boundaries it may be wise to take along another person such as a spouse or colleague, or to ask the parishoner to ask a friend or member of the congregation to be present. Whether or not to continue with crisis counseling or to refer is a decision that must be made in such a way as to protect the counselee and to maintain the primary role responsibilities of the minister.

If the *who* is a child or adolescent member, or only one spouse of a couple relationship, then appropriate boundary setting requires recognizing that there is also a pastoral relationship that must be maintained with the parent(s) of the child or adolescent member, or with the other spouse if seeing only one person from a marriage. To fail to remember those other relationships places the minister at risk of allowing a counseling ministry to render the minister ineffective in other more primary roles.

The *what,* of course, is pastoral counseling, although as earlier noted, it may be more appropriate to refer counseling and to respond rather with short-term, supportive pastoral care. Classic texts such as Howard

Clinebell's *Basic Types of Pastoral Counseling* can be helpful in discerning the types of counseling ministry that can be compatible with your particular ministry. Generally speaking, sexual counseling or therapy is not appropriate to be provided by a parish pastor, other than the very basic education that is involved in pre-marital counseling or the simplest of marital questions. In some states, such as Florida, it is unethical for even a marriage and family therapist to do sexual counseling unless they have advanced training and certification from a professional association such as the American Association of Sex Educators, Counselors, and Therapists.

Where pastoral care takes place is often dictated by the nature of the need. A hospital E.R. or patient room, a convalescent or nursing home, a funeral home, the parishoner's home, or the church are very common contexts for supportive pastoral ministry. If, however, the minister chooses to do counseling, there needs to be a balance of concern for privacy and confidentiality and the maintenance of appropriate boundaries that safeguard the vulnerabilities and reputations of both the counselee and the minister. Extended or frequent counseling sessions in a parishoner's home are unwise, except in highly unusual circumstances. In those situations other safeguards can be put in place. For example, the minister could be certain to wear clerical clothing or whatever would be traditional attire for that denomination's official functioning when doing counseling in a private home. Also, if someone were confined to bed at home there could be a family member or friend asked to be in another room. In addition, time boundaries could be decided ahead of time and the church office manager or the minister's spouse or a friend be alerted to a problematic counseling situation and the time boundaries that have been established. The visit may also be documented in the pastor's confidential parish files.

When to counsel? Counseling that takes place in the church building would wisely be scheduled at a time when there are persons other than the counselee also in the church building, such as the church office manager or other staff member. When possible without compromising confidentiality, the door of the room where counseling is taking place might be left slightly open. In this day of increased awareness of clergy sexual abuse, paying attention to the *where* and *when* of counseling serves as a reminder both to the counselee and the minister that appropriate boundaries are vital to healing and will be maintained.

The *how* of counseling, if the minister chooses to do any counseling other than supportive pastoral care, might prudently include training and then regular supervision from a professional counselor. A local AAPC fellow or diplomate, or CPE chaplain could provide that kind of supervision, as well as community psychologists, social workers, or other licensed mental health counselors known to the minister as being sensitive to religious issues and supportive of religious leaders. Such supervision would provide an additional opportunity to consider what kinds of counseling approaches might be helpful, and when referral to a professional counselor would be even more helpful. For those who want to do no harm, regular supervision is an additional safeguard. Commitment to regular supervision of any form of ministry where there is increased risk to a parishoner and increased vulnerability for the minister indicates concern on the part of the minister to be ethical and faithful.

NOTES

Chapter 1

1. Old Testament theologian Walter Eichrodt, for example, structured his entire work around the theme of covenant. This focus on covenant in Old Testament studies was propelled by the discoveries during the earlier decades of this century of a number of ancient Near Eastern treaty documents written between one king and another that made and sealed international agreements. Since a number of these treaty or covenant documents were dated some 1,000 years before the Exodus event itself, there seems to be ample proof that Israel was heir to a long tradition of written treaties. Furthermore, scholars who studied these treaties in detail isolated what they described as a characteristic literary "treaty pattern." When this pattern was held up against the literary character of certain Old Testament writings, especially the Decalogue or Ten Commandments, a correspondence was noted. It was argued that this literary treaty pattern was the basis for the composition of considerable portions of the biblical material, and that the concept of treaty or covenant was central to the biblical way of thinking theologically.

There are those who question whether the term "covenant" can bear this weight. Therefore, the other side of the argument is that the term "treaty" or "covenant"—the Hebrew word *berit*—is remarkably absent from much of Israel's literature, especially the literature of the earliest prophetic writings. Most notably, German scholar Lothar Perlitt attacked the thesis that Israel thought of its relation with God as a sort of treaty or covenant arrangement. Perlitt and others have noted that the word "covenant" is scarcely used at all in Amos, Hosea, Isaiah, and Micah. In fact, Perlitt argued, it was only in relatively *later* writings that Israel began to think of its relationship with God as a sort of covenant or treaty. Treaty language first begins showing up in what scholars have come to refer to as Deuteronomistic writings, especially in the Deuteronomistically edited form of the book of Deuteronomy. Such Deuteronomistic editing and writing was generally associated with the period of King Josiah in the seventh century—or even later, during the subsequent exile of Judah in Babylon during the sixth century. These scholars argued, therefore, that the notion of covenant was a relatively late idea that intruded its way into Israelite theological reflection, and could therefore not be regarded as a central concept that drove Israel's theological thought forward from its earliest days.

2. In addition, a concept related to covenant, election, was indeed central to Israel's self-understanding. Deuteronomy 32:8 rehearses what must have been a very early understanding of how the seventy nations of the world were divided up among the seventy gods, with the result that Jacob is allotted to Yahweh as his portion. In the same way, Jud. 11:21-24 recalls an argument between Jephthah, one of Israel's Judges, and the Ammonites in which Jephthah argues that the territory of Ammon belongs to Chemosh and the territory of Israel belongs to Yahweh.

3. Early epic traditions about Abraham and Sarah and their descendants made the rather bold step of thinking of this election in terms derived from the custom of one king making a treaty or covenant with another king (Genesis 15). Under the influence of Deuteronomic theology, this concept of covenant gradually came to symbolize Israel's theology of election, so that by the time of the Josianic reformation in the seventh century B.C.E. it was quite common for those such as Jeremiah to think in terms of an old covenant and a new one to be established in God's eschatological future (cf. Jer. 11:1-13 and 31:31-34). See also Frank H. Seilhamer, *Here Am I: A Study of the Presence of God in the Old Testament and in the Writings of Luther* (Lima, Ohio: C.S.S. Publishing Co., 1972).

4. Mark Galli, "Leadership at Its Best," *Leadership* (Winter, 1990), 41-47.

5. In 1982 Craig Ellison reported the results of a survey of 1,000 *Leadership* readers, briefly summarized in "Where Does It Hurt?" *Leadership* (Spring, 1982).

6. Donald C. Houts, "Pastoral Care for Pastors: Toward a Church Strategy," *Pastoral Psychology*, 25/3 (1977), 186-96, came to similar conclusions, says Craig W. Ellison and William S. Mattila, "with a greater emphasis on loneliness, expectations, feelings of inadequacy, and a lost sense of meaning."

7. Stephen Daniel and Martha L. Rogers, "Burnout and the Pastorate: A Critical Review with Implications for Pastors," *Journal of Psychology and Theology*, 9/3 (1981), 232-49, reviewed the literature about burnout and found many of the variables "include stress from constant interpersonal contact and continually increasing effort to meet the rigorous demands and expectations. Houts (n. 6) also identified expectations as an issue.

8. Ibid. There is a fuller discussion of the survey results in Craig W. Ellison and William S. Mattila, "The Needs of Evangelical Christian Leaders in the United States," *Journal of Psychology and Theology* 11/1 (1983), 28-35.

9. John Keller, *Let Go, Let God* (Minneapolis: Augsburg Publishing House, 1985).

10. David Goetz, "Is the Pastor's Family Safe at Home?" *Leadership* (Fall, 1992), 39-44.

11. Roy Oswald, *How to Build a Support System for Your Ministry* (Washington, D. C.: The Alban Institute, 1991).

12. The guidelines and sample covenant in this chapter are verbatim or adapted from the Colleague 2 Program (John L. Davis, editor and Dorothy Williams, writer),

originally administered by William C. Behrens for the ELCA. Materials are available through Dick Bruesehoff, Director for Leadership Support, Division for Ministry, Evangelical Lutheran Church in America (ELCA), 8765 W. Higgins Road, Chicago, Ill. 60631-4198.

Chapter 2

13. Specifics and details of counseling appointments should not be shared in order to not compromise confidentiality. For guidance in this area it is best to seek consultation or supervision with a certified pastoral counselor or other licensed counselor while keeping in mind that, even then, the identity of individuals must be kept confidential. How could Leon use this group as a sounding board for talking about the situation with Flo?

14. Frederick Buechner, *Wishful Thinking: A Theological ABC* (New York: Harper and Row, 1973).

15. John D. Vogelsang, "Reconstructing the Response to Clergy Sexual Abuse," p. 11, a paper distributed by Division for Ministry, ELCA (see n. 12).

16. George Keck, *Mutual Ministry Committee: A Vision for Building Up the Body of Christ*, p. 5, available through Leadership Support, Division for Ministry, ELCA.

17. "The Church's One Foundation," *Lutheran Book of Worship* (Minneapolis: Augsburg Publishing House, 1978), Hymn 369.

18. Edwin Friedman, *Generation to Generation* (New York: Guilford Publications, 1986) and Peter Steinke, *How Your Church Family Works* (Washington, D.C.: Alban Publications, 1995).

Chapter 3

19. Gary L. Harbaugh, *Caring for the Caregiver* (Washington, D.C.: Alban Publications), 1992.

20. Gary L. Harbaugh, *Pastor as Person* (Minneapolis: Augsburg Publishing House, 1984), David Ostergren cited on p. 153.

21. Carol Gilligan, *In a Different Voice* (Cambridge, Mass.: Harvard University Press, 1982), explores psychological theory and women's development.

22. Rosemary Radford Ruether, *Women-Church* (San Francisco: Harper & Row, 1985).

23. Recent books dealing with ethical issues in ministry include Jan Erikson-Pearson, *Safe Connections: What Parishioners Can Do to Understand and Prevent Clergy Sexual Abuse* (Chicago: Division for Ministry, ELCA, 1996) and Pamela Cooper-White, *The Cry of Tamar: Violence against Women and the Church's Response* (Minneapolis: Fortress Press, 1995).

24. Cf. G. M. Atkinson and D. W. Sue, "A Cross-Cultural Perspective," *Counseling American Minorities*, 3d ed., 1989, and M. J. Gold, C. A. Grant and H. Riulin, *In Praise of Diversity: A Resource Book for Multicultural Education*, 1977, cited in the *Leader's*

Guide for the Colleague Program, Chicago, Evangelical Lutheran Church in America, Nov. 1, 1995, p. 34., based on the participant's manual at the Multicultural Education and Training Institutes (MET), (ELCA, Chicago, October 1990.)

25. David Goetz, "Is the Pastor's Family Safe at Home?" *Leadership* (Fall, 1992), 39-44; Donald Houts, "Pastoral Care for Pastors: Toward a Church Strategy," *Pastoral Psychology* 25/3 (1977), 186-96; Stephen Daniel and Martha L. Rogers, "Burn-out and the Pastorate: A Critical Review with Implications for Pastors," *Journal of Psychology and Theology* 9/3 (1981), 232-49.

26. Ibid. Cf. Craig W. Ellison and William S. Mattila, "The Needs of Evangelical Christian Leaders in the United States," *Journal of Psychology and Theology*, Vol. 11/ 1 (1983), 28-35.

27. Ibid.

28. This vision of the covenant made with Moses at Sinai was central to what is referred to as the Deuteronomic and Deuteronomistic traditions. Unlike the earlier tradition concerning God's covenant with Abraham and Sarah, which arose in the midst of Israel's initial euphoria and gave expression to its unbridled optimism, this later Deuteronomic tradition emerged from the lengthy period of crisis in Israel's corporate life. The euphoria had waned, the political realities had set in, Israel was torn asunder, dividing into competing northern and southern kingdoms, both kingdoms coming increasingly under the domination of the opportunistic empire of Assyria to the east. Trade languished, economic security crumbled, morale collapsed, and, what was the worst from the perspective of these Deuteronomic circles, Israel slid into religious apostasy. The covenant with Moses is painted in dark tones reflecting the pessimism and heaviness which characterized Israel's slow decline in the face of a changing world. It provided the basis on which the prophets would unleash their bittersweet rendition of Israel's life with God, a life marked primarily by divine fidelity in the midst of miserable human failure.

29. Dietrich Bonhoeffer, *The Cost of Discipleship* (New York: MacMillan Publishing Co., 1963).

30. Gary L. Harbaugh, *Pastor as Person*, pp. 18ff., citing J. A. T. Robinson in T. A. Kantonen, *Life after Death* (Philadelphia: Fortress Press, 1962).

31. Gary L. Harbaugh, *Pastor as Person*, p. 155, citing Chaplain Carl Nighswonger. A contemporary expression of the God-question is the memorable way it is posed by Lutheran Theological Southern Seminary pastoral care colleague Dr. Daryll (Tony) Everett: WIGIAT, which stands for "Where is God in all this?"

32. Gary L. Harbaugh, *Pastor as Person*, p. 19; cf. Ezekiel 36:26.

Chapter 4

33. When the Deuteronomistic historian speaks of God making a promise to David he is casting David in a real sense as a new Abraham. Just as Abraham is promised a perpetual family, so is David. David points to the Mosaic covenant as Israel's king stands under the thumb of Israel's torah tradition.

34. Gary L. Harbaugh, *Pastor as Person*, pp. 21-29, details Erik Erikson's developmental stages. Cf. Donald Capps, *Pastoral Care: A Thematic Approach* (Philadelphia:

Westminster Press, 1979) and *The Life Cycle and Pastoral Care* (Philadelphia: Fortress Press, 1983). Also, Don S. Browning, *Generative Man: Psychoanalytic Perspectives* (Philadelphia: Westminster Press, 1973).

35. Mary Field Belenky, Blythe McVicker Clinchy, Nancy Rule Goldberger, and Jill Mattuck Tarule, *Women's Ways of Knowing: The Development of Self, Voice, and Mind* (New York: Basic Books, 1986).

36. Carol Gilligan, *In a Different Voice*, p. 171.

37. Murray Bowen is one of the leading family systems theorists. Murray Bowen and Michael Kerr, *Family Evaluation: An Approach Based on Bowen Theory* (New York: W. W. Norton & Company, 1988).

38. Ibid.

39. Marianne Walters, Betty Carter, Peggy Papp, and Olga Silverstein, *The Invisible Web: Gender Patterns in Family Relationships* (New York: Guilford Press, 1988).

Chapter 5

40. Gary L. Harbaugh, *God's Gifted People* (Minneapolis: Augsburg Books), 1990, p. 100.

41. Ibid.

42. Martin Luther, "Small Catechism," *Book of Concord*, T. G. Tappert, ed. (Philadelphia: Fortress Press, 1959).

43. Gary L. Harbaugh and Evan Rogers, "Pastoral Burn-out: A View from the Seminary," *Journal of Pastoral Care* 38/2 (1984), 99-106.

44. Marsha Wiggins Frame and Constance L. Shehan, "Work and Well-Being in the Two-Person Career: Relocation Stress and Coping Among Clergy Husbands and Wives," *Family Relations* (April, 1994), 1-10.

45. Gary L. Harbaugh, *The Faith-Hardy Christian* (Minneapolis: Augsburg Publishing House), 1986, and Gary L. Harbaugh and Evan Rogers, "Pastoral Burn-out: A View from the Seminary," *Journal of Pastoral Care* 38/2 (1984), 99-106.

Chapter 6

46. Kenneth Kaugk, *Antagonists in the Church: How to Identify and Deal with Destructive Conflict* (Minneapolis: Augsburg, 1988).

47. Arlin Rothauge, *Sizing Up a Congregation for New Member Ministry* summarized in Roy M. Oswald, "Moving from One Size Church to Another," Alban Institute, 1990.

48. (*chozeh* and *ro'eh*).

49. Gary L. Harbaugh, *The Faith-hardy Christian*; "The Person in Ministry," *Trinity Seminary Review* (Spring, 1983) 3-13; *Pastor as Person*; Gary L. Harbaugh and Evan Rogers, "Pastoral Burn-out: A View from the Seminary," *Journal of Pastoral Care* 38/2 (1984), 99-106; Gary L. Harbaugh and William C. Behrens, "The Pastor's Spouse: Hurts, Hopes and Helps," *Trinity Seminary Review* (Fall, 1984), 36-40.

50. Stephen Daniel and Martha L. Rogers, "Burn-out and the Pastorate: A Critical Review with Implications for Pastors," *Journal of Psychology and Theology* 9/3 (1981), 232-249).

51. Fred Smith, "The Care and Feeding of Critics: How to Feed the Hand that Bites

You," *Leadership* (Winter, 1995), 29-35.

52. Ibid.

53. Ibid. There are other good suggestions given in the article, such as, limit the criticism you'll accept; make constructive criticism part of the culture; don't turn criticism into a personal contest; admit when you've been wrong; and don't take revenge.

54. Transitions Seminar materials, Division for Ministry, Leadership Support, ELCA, Chicago, Illinois (see n. 12).

Chapter 7

55. Peter Rutter, *Sex in the Forbidden Zone* (Los Angeles: Jeremy P. Tarcher, Inc., 1989), p. 46.

56. Marilyn R. Peterson, "Prevention: Developing Boundary Awareness and Decision Making Across Professional Disciplines," p. 1.

57. Marie M. Fortune, *Is Nothing Sacred? When Sex Invades the Pastoral Relationship* (San Francisco: Harper & Row, 1989), Appendix, p. 135.

58. Marie M. Fortune, Center for the Prevention of Sexual and Domestic Violence, 936 N. 34th Street, Suite 200, Seattle, Wash. 98103.

59. Ibid. Cf. Peter Rutter, *Sex in the Forbidden Zone*, p. 48.

60. Ibid., pp. 23, 24. State laws prohibit the violation of the sexual boundaries of clients by professionals. For example, Florida State Law (Chapter 21CC-10.001) rules it unethical and unlawful for psychotherapists to violate the sexual boundary in a professional relationship and recognizes that "the effects of the psychotherapist-client relationship are powerful and subtle and that clients are influenced consciously and subconsciously by the unequal distribution of power inherent in such relationships. . . . Client(s) should be irrebuttably presumed incapable of giving valid, informed, free consent to sexual activity involving the psychotherapist."

61. Marie M. Fortune, an ordained minister of the United Church of Christ, is the founder and executive director of The Center for the Prevention of Sexual and Domestic Violence. Publications by Marie Fortune include: *Is Nothing Sacred? When Sex Invades the Pastoral Relationship*; *Violence in the Family—A Workshop Curriculum for Clergy and Other Helpers*; *Keeping The Faith: Questions and Answers for the Abused Woman*; and *Love Does No Harm: Sexual Ethics For The Rest of Us*. The efforts of the Center are centered in the religious community: training clergy and lay leaders to deal with the problems; helping those with questions find appropriate assistance; and helping to change the fundamental beliefs and practices which allow abuse to continue. The Center uplifts the concerns of Susan Schecter in her book *Women and Male Violence*: "The battered are enormously relieved to hear a trusted institution (like the Church) publicly articulate that violence against them is wrong and not to be endured." For further information and resources write: the Center for the Prevention of Sexual and Domestic Violence, 936 N. 34th Street, Suite 200 Seattle, Wash. 98103; phone (206)634-1903.

62. Dennis T. Olson, "Journey Toward Jericho," *Saints and Sojourners* (Minneapolis: Augsburg Books, 1990), p. 47.

63. American Association for Marriage and Family Therapy (AAMFT) code of ethics.

64. Center for Prevention Workshop Manual, p. 35; see n. 61.

65. Karen Strohm Kitchener and Susan Stefanowski Harding, "Dual Role Relationships," in Larry B. Golden and Barbara Herlihy, *Ethical Standards Casebook* (Alexandria, Va.: American Association for Counseling and Development, 1990), pp. 52-153.

66. Israel connected the prophet with certain professional competencies and the priest with others, and these two areas were designated by the terms "word" (*dabar*) and "instruction" (*tora*). One of the earliest witnesses to the priest's role in society is the Song of Moses in which Moses blesses each of the tribes, bequeathing upon it its identity. Of the tribe of Levi it is said, "Give to Levi your Thummim, and your Urim to your loyal one.... May they teach Jacob your ordinances and Israel your law; may they place incense before you and whole burnt offerings on your altar" (Deut. 33:8-10). There are three areas of competency listed above, that associated with Urim and Thummim, with instruction, and with sacrifice.

67. The theory that there was a natural hatred that existed between prophets and priests in Israel, that they had some sort of genetic predisposition to loath one another, is simply incorrect. The prophet never criticizes the priest for being a priest. The prophet only criticizes the priest when he *ceases* to be a priest and gives up his responsibility to the torah. Whenever the priest fails in the responsibility to be the protector and instructor of Israel's torah tradition, it is *then* that the priest comes under prophetic censure.

68. Walter Brueggemann, *The Creative Word: Canon as a Model for Biblical Education* (Philadelphia: Fortress Press, 1982), pp. 20-21, 35.

69. Torah was not simply a legal code, but rather a symbol for a comprehensive way of viewing religious truth. We recall that the responsibility of the prophet was the divine "word" that came to the prophet intuitively and with shocking immediacy. The prophet was inspired to stretch the people's mythic consciousness, sometimes to the breaking point. The priest, however was responsible for torah, an essentially inductive enterprise in which the priest searched through material evidence for divine truth. Whether a cow's liver or a handful of arrows, whether Urim and Thummim or the scroll of the Torah. The priest was the one who had hands on approach to religious truth.

70. Rodney R. Hutton, *Charisma and Authority in Israelite Society* (Minneapolis: Fortress Press, 1994), pp. 170-71.

71. The word they used to describe this order is *tsedaqah*, or "righteousness". They could even refer to the continuous "mighty deeds" of God on behalf of Israel as the *tsidqot YHWH*, or the "righteous deeds of the Lord." The very heavens and the structure of the cosmos were viewed to be imbued and saturated with God's justice and righteousness. Present reality was not the result of countless chance occurrences. It was rather the result of God's just and righteous will, which filled every crevice and crack of creation.

72. The Reverend Paul Harms, professor of homiletics at Trinity Lutheran Seminary, uses this example of the proclamation of law and gospel.

73. Examples of denominational policies are included in Marie Fortune's book, *Is Nothing Sacred?* (see n. 61). Excellent suggestions for preventing sexual boundary violations appear in Part 5 of Jan Erikson-Pearson's *Safe Connections* (see n. 23). *Safe Connections* also contains an annotated bibliography of relevant books and videos.

74. Sheryl C. Fancher, Midwest Career Development Center, 754 No. 31st Street, Kansas City, Mo. 66110.

75. *Sexual Misconduct—Sexual Abuse in the Ministerial Relationship,* Trainer's Manual, p. 30, Center for Prevention (see n. 61).

76. Additional resources for understanding the dynamics of sexual abuse and guidelines for pastoral care include: *The Courage To Heal: A Guide for Women Survivors of Child Sexual Abuse,* by Ellen Bass and Laura Davis (New York: Harper & Row, 1988); *Allies in Healing: A Support Book For Partners,* by Laura Davis (New York: Harper-Collins, 1991); and *Sexual Violence, The Unmentionable Sin: An Ethical and Pastoral Perspective,* by Marie M. Fortune (New York: The Pilgrim Press, 1983). An excellent resource on domestic violence is: *Violence in the Family: A Workshop Curriculum for Clergy and Other Helpers,* by Marie M. Fortune of The Center for the Prevention of Sexual and Domestic Violence (Cleveland: Pilgrim Press, 1991).

77. Many women ministers report having experienced boundary violations prior to their ordination. After ordination, female ministers continue to contend with the possibility of sexual exploitation, including exploitation by their parishoners.

Karen Lebacqz and Ronald G. Barton in *Sex In The Parish* (Louisville: Westminster/John Knox Press, 1991), p. 135, write: "Male pastors are concerned about protecting female parishioners from unprofessional advances. Female pastors are concerned about protecting themselves. The difference is striking." Women ministers often find useful a peer group of other female professionals in learning to set and maintain clear boundaries. It is helpful to hear how others have responded to a subtle or direct invitation to cross ethical boundaries. For ongoing healing of past violations and support as minorities in the workplace, peer groups prove to be beneficial.

We also note that male ministers experience sexual exploitation in the parish and in society, although incidents are not reported as frequently. In regards to the physical, emotional, sexual abuse of males, more health care professionals are concluding that the cases of abuse reported are significantly lower than the actual number of men who have been abused. It is believed that we will see an increase in reporting by males who have been abused due to more information available about domestic violence in general and more permission given from social groups for males in particular to come forward.

Chapter 8

78. Gary L. Harbaugh, *God's Gifted People.* Other important discussions of the sixteen MBTI psychological types include those by Mary McCaulley, Sandra Hirsch, Jean Kummerow, Gordon Lawrence, Isabel Briggs Myers, Judith Provost, Naomi Quenk, Flavil Yeakley, and other members of the faculty of the Association for Psychological

Type. Resource materials and training programs are available through the Center for Applications of Psychological Type, 2720 N. W. 6th St., Gainesville, Fla. 32609; the Association for Psychological Type, 9140 Ward Parkway, Kansas City, Mo. 64114; Consulting Psychologists Press, 577 College Avenue, Palo Alto, Cal. 94306; and Type Resources, Inc., 101 Chestnut St. #135, Gaithersburg, Md. 20877.

79. This anti-royalist perspective can be seen lying not far beneath Samuel's words of warning to the people that the king would conscript their sons for military service and the king would surround himself with a huge bureaucracy to tend the ever expanding royal appetite and lust for power (1 Sam. 8:10-18).

80. Where such customs of anointing originally came from is highly debated. The verb *mashach* has as its basic meaning "to smear", and in its earliest usage it is associated with smearing oil on shields in preparation for warfare (Isa. 21:5). Therefore, when it is reported that King Saul had been slain on the battlefield, it is lamented that his shield was "anointed with oil no more" (2 Sam. 1:21). Though never stated, the underlying notion may have been that the smearing of the oil on shields and other utensils was done in order to lend them a certain inviolability, making them impervious to attack and impenetrable by arrows and spears.

81. Gary L. Harbaugh, *Pastor as Person*, pp. 134f.

82. Gary L. Harbaugh, "Surviving and Thriving in Ministry," Academy of Parish Clergy.

83. John Keller, *Let Go, Let God* (Minneapolis: Augsburg Publishing House, 1985).

Chapter 9

84. David Livingstone, in Frederick J. Schumacher, ed., with Dorothy A. Zelenko, *For All the Saints: A Prayer Book for and by the Church*, Vol. 3 (Delhi, N.Y.: The American Lutheran Publicity Bureau, 1995), p. 244; Cf. Gary L. Harbaugh, "An Act of God," *The Lutheran*, October 1993, for an explication of ministry issues in disaster situations.

85. *Vision and Expectations*, Ordained Ministers in the ELCA, 1990, ELCA, adopted by Church Council of the ELCA, October 1990, p. 5.

86. Attributed to Martin Luther.

87. Luther's explanation of the Third Article of the Apostles Creed.

88. Henri Nouwen, *Reaching Out* (New York: Doubleday, 1975), p. 89.

89. Margaret A. Farley, *Personal Commitments: Beginning, Keeping, Changing* (San Francisco: Harper & Row, 1986), p. 116.

90. Walter Wangerin, "A Meditation on Marriage," January 14, 1996, "Lutheran Vespers."

91. Margaret A. Farley, *Personal Commitments: Beginning, Keeping, Changing*, p. 133.

92. ELCA service of ordination, see n. 12.

93. *Occasional Services: A Companion to the Lutheran Book of Worship*, p. 197.

94. George Keck, Mutual Ministry booklet, see n. 16.

95. ELCA *Vision and Expectations*, p. 11. The ELCA (Craig Settlage and Steve Ganzkow-Wold) and LCMS (Bruce Hartung) are developing additional programs and

resources to support ministerial health and wellness. Cf. n. 12.

96. Ibid. , p. 13.

97. Marie R. Fortune, *Love Does No Harm*, pp. 128-32.

98. Margaret A. Farley, *Personal Commitments: Beginning, Keeping, Changing*, p. 30. For another perspective on relationships, see Lewis Tagliaferre, *Kisses Aren't Contracts* (Salt Lake City: Northwest Publishing, Inc., in publication).

99. Margaret A. Farley, *Personal Commitments: Beginning, Keeping, Changing*, p. 18.

100. Walter Wangerin, "A Meditation on Marriage," January 14, 1996, on "Lutheran Vespers" radio ministry, ELCA, Chicago.

101. Margaret A. Farley, *Personal Commitments: Beginning, Keeping, Changing*, p. 110.

Chapter 10

102. ATS "Readiness for Ministry" research by the Association of Theological Schools. See also, David S. Schuler, M. P. Strommen, M. Brekke, eds., *Ministry in America* (San Francisco: Harper & Row, 1980).

103. Gary L. Harbaugh, *Pastor as Person*, p. 156.

104. Cynthia Jurrison, presentation for the Conference of Bishops, Evangelical Lutheran Church in America, at Mundelein, Ill., 1996.

105. Ralph Sockman, "The Meaning of Suffering," in Frederick J. Schumacher, ed., with Dorothy A. Zelenko, *For All the Saints: A Prayer Book for and by the Church*, Vol. III, p. 272.

106. Luther's explanation to Third Article of the Apostle's Creed

107. Cynthia Jurrison and Timothy Lull, both presenters at the Conference of Bishops, ELCA, see n. 104.

108. Martin Luther, *The Book of Concord*, in Frederick J. Schumacher, ed., with Dorothy A. Zelenko, *For All the Saints: A Prayer Book for and by the Church*, vol. 3, p. 343.

109. Gary L. Harbaugh, *The Faith-Hardy Christian*. See n. 49.

110. Gary L. Harbaugh, *God's Gifted People*, p. 100.

111. Walter R. Bouman and Sue M. Setzer, *What Shall I Say: Discerning God's Call to Ministry* (Chicago: Evangelical Lutheran Church in America, 1995).

112. Gary L. Harbaugh, *God's Gifted People*.

113. Ralph W. Sockman, *The Meaning of Suffering*, cited in Frederick J. Schumacher, ed., with Dorothy A. Zelenko, *For All the Saints: A Prayer Book for and by the Church*, vol. 3, p. 272.

114. *Lutheran Book of Worship*, p. 137.

115. Paul Sherer, "The Ageless Cross," in Frederick J. Schumacher, ed., with Dorothy A. Zelenko, *For All the Saints: A Prayer Book for and by the Church*, Vol. III, p. 1007.

INDEX